Beneath the Surface: Echoes from Beth Israel Cemetery

The Grave Whisperer

Angeline Gallant

Published by Angeline Gallant, 2024.

While every precaution has been taken in the preparation of this book, the publisher assumes no responsibility for errors or omissions, or for damages resulting from the use of the information contained herein.

BENEATH THE SURFACE: ECHOES FROM BETH ISRAEL CEMETERY

First edition. October 28, 2024.

ISBN: 979-8223453000

Written by Angeline Gallant.

Also by Angeline Gallant

A Dragon's Diary
Dreaming of Dragons

Calling Her Heart
Whisper of the Heart
No Turning Back
Forsake Me Not
Hear My Cry

FORGET ME NOT
Victoria, Ontario's Babies 1894 - 1895

GENERATIONS OF THE VOLGA
A Family's Legacy

Guardian of the Heart
Fallen Petals

Keeper Of Secrets
A Lady's Secret

Kingston's Love Chronicles
Springtime Promises

Midnight's Awakening
Heart of the Storm
Walking Through The Storm
Walking Through The Storm
Heart of the Storm

Secrets of the Underworld
Deklan's Dragons

Tell My Story Collection
Tell My Story: Germany 1851
Tell My Story: England 1852
Whispers From The Garrison Church

The Dervock Legacy
Echoes of Dervock

The Wolf Whisperer volumes 1 & 2

Timeless
The Time Keeper's Sanctuary

Timeless Whispers of Dervock Saga
Secrets of Dervock

Standalone
Winds of Change vol 1-3

Watch for more at https://www.goodreads.com/author/show/
19703964.Angeline_Gallant.

Table of Contents

Doris (Kizell) Berofe[1]

Doris Kizell's story immediately takes me back to the small, close-knit community of Killaloe, Ontario, in the early 20th century—a place marked by its simple charm and the strength of its people. Born in October 1921, Doris grew up at a time when the world was in flux, especially for the Jewish communities across North America. It must have been both comforting and challenging to be part of a Jewish family in such a rural Canadian setting, where the traditions of her faith and culture would have set her apart in ways that could be isolating yet deeply enriching.

I imagine Doris's childhood might have been filled with unique customs, family gatherings around religious holidays, and a steadfast sense of community among the Jewish families in Killaloe. Back then, the Jewish population in small Canadian towns wasn't large, so each family carried a vital piece of their heritage. Doris's life would have been shaped not only by the landscapes of Killaloe but also by the resilience and unity of her community, striving to preserve their cultural and religious identity amid an ever-changing world.

Doris's birthdate, October 1921, also places her in a fascinating historical context. She would have been a young woman during World War II, and given her heritage, the war years likely held special significance for her and her family. The war, no doubt, brought awareness of global events painfully close to home, reinforcing her Jewish identity while underscoring the challenges facing Jews worldwide.

If you were to delve further, you may be able to explore the Kizell family records, perhaps discovering immigration papers, family stories, or even recipes passed down from one generation to the next. Genealogy isn't just about tracing names on a tree; it's about unearthing the rich tapestry of one's heritage, piecing together the joys and struggles that shaped each generation. Doris's story is a reminder of how each life, each name, carries the weight of the past and the promise of continuity.

DORIS'S RETURN TO OTTAWA at just 10 months old in 1922 adds a compelling layer to her story, hinting that her early life was already touched by travel and perhaps by the echoes of family connections or responsibilities overseas. That period marked a time of immense movement and resettlement, especially for Jewish families who sought better lives, often reuniting with relatives abroad or returning after visiting family members. Her parents may have taken her abroad to introduce her to extended family, bringing her back to Ottawa with the hope of planting roots in a growing city where there were more opportunities for work, education, and community.

Ottawa in the 1920s was a place where the Jewish community was beginning to establish stronger footholds, building synagogues and community centers that served as social and spiritual hubs. For Doris, Ottawa would be where she grew up and where she absorbed not just her heritage, but also the broader Canadian culture and values. Her family's presence in Ottawa likely connected her to other Jewish families who shared similar stories of resilience, journeys across oceans, and the challenge of maintaining their heritage while embracing their Canadian identity.

As a genealogist, I wonder about the records that might exist from that early journey, such as passenger manifests or immigration documents, which could reveal more about the family's origins and connections. Perhaps they carried with them items that symbolized their heritage—a menorah, family photos, letters, or religious texts—all treasures that reinforced their identity in a new land. Doris's return to Canada at such a tender age speaks to the hope her parents likely held for her future, one where she could grow up safely and freely, in a country that could become her lifelong home.

Doris's story would grow from this return to Ottawa, branching out into school friendships, early ambitions, and the richness of a life shaped by both her Jewish identity and her Canadian upbringing. I can't help but imagine that her early travels imprinted a sense of connection to the world beyond Canada's borders—a heritage she would carry forward, honoring her family's past while building her future.

WHEN DORIS WAS JUST two years old, her little brother, Raymond Harold, was born on January 26, 1924. I can picture Doris, a toddler herself, peering curiously into the cradle where her new sibling lay—a moment that would mark the beginning of a lifelong sibling bond. Raymond's arrival would have brought new energy and excitement into the Kizell household. Being the older sister, even by a couple of years, would give Doris a special place in Raymond's life, and likely, in her family's story.

As the Kizells settled into their life in Ottawa, the 1920s roared on around them, a time of social change and growth, especially in cities like Ottawa, where Jewish communities were becoming more established and thriving in the cultural mosaic of Canadian society. Doris and Raymond would grow up amid this setting, one that blended their Jewish traditions with the progressive currents of Canadian life, while facing the unique pressures that came with being Jewish in a largely Christian society. It must have been an interesting, sometimes challenging balance for their parents, raising their children to be proud of their heritage while adapting to their new home.

As she grew, Doris would likely take on the role of a guide and playmate to Raymond, teaching him the small lessons of childhood. The pair might have attended school together, shared family celebrations, and even squabbled, as siblings do, over toys or the attention of their parents. The 1930s and '40s would bring new phases of life as they both came of age during a time of economic hardship, followed by the turmoil of World War II. Ottawa's Jewish community, which was resilient and tight-knit, would have been a source of strength for the Kizells as they navigated these difficult times.

The relationship between Doris and Raymond would have grown even stronger with the years, forged by shared experiences, their Jewish heritage, and the values passed down from their parents. For Doris, having Raymond as her little brother would be a lifelong bond, likely filled with cherished memories and family traditions. This era of Doris's life, growing up in Ottawa with Raymond by her side, paints a picture of a family committed to their heritage, finding a place in Canada while preserving the legacy they carried from overseas. In the larger tapestry of their lives, Raymond's birth was one more stitch in a rich family history that continued to evolve in their new home.

WHEN DORIS WAS THREE years old, her family welcomed another sibling—her sister, Greta, born on July 11, 1925. This addition to the Kizell family must have transformed their home, making it livelier and filled with even more love, laughter, and the inevitable dynamics of sibling relationships. As the eldest, Doris would naturally become a little caretaker, guiding both Raymond and Greta as they grew up together, the three siblings forming a close trio.

With two younger siblings, Doris's role in the family would likely deepen. She may have felt a sense of responsibility to watch over Raymond and Greta, becoming a comforting presence for them both.

Growing up, the Kizell children would have shared many childhood experiences and memories—playing together, exploring the streets of Ottawa, and celebrating Jewish holidays as a family. Greta, being closer in age to Doris than Raymond, would perhaps look up to her sister, following her lead as they navigated childhood together.

In Ottawa, the family would have been surrounded by a supportive Jewish community, helping the siblings feel a sense of belonging in a country where they were part of a minority. Doris, Raymond, and Greta would have grown up celebrating holidays like Hanukkah and Passover together, learning the stories, songs, and traditions from their parents. These traditions, likely passed down from previous generations, would help bind them not only as siblings but as members of the larger Jewish community.

The late 1920s and early 1930s would bring both joy and challenges. As the Great Depression unfolded, families across Canada faced financial and social difficulties. For the Kizells, it would have been a time of tightening belts and finding strength in each other. Doris, the eldest, may have even taken on small chores to help her parents or to keep her younger siblings entertained during tough times. Despite the hardships, her family's unity and faith would have been constants, providing a foundation of resilience that Doris would carry throughout her life.

Together, Doris, Raymond, and Greta would share countless experiences—from childhood games to teenage adventures, and ultimately, they would enter adulthood with a rich tapestry of shared memories. Each new addition to the family, each birth, and every new story woven into their lives would shape Doris's story, making her journey richer and more deeply connected to her heritage and to the family that shaped her.

BY 1931, DORIS WAS nine years old, firmly rooted in her childhood and living in Ottawa with her family, a bustling and vibrant city with a growing Jewish community. As the eldest of the three Kizell children, she would have been starting to find her own place in the family, old enough to help with tasks around the house and young enough to still enjoy the innocent wonders of childhood.

Ottawa during this time offered an interesting environment for Jewish families like the Kizells. With Canada feeling the effects of the Great Depression, times were tough, and families faced economic uncertainty. For Jewish communities in Ottawa, the Depression years also saw an increase in resilience and unity, as they leaned on each other for support. Doris's parents may have had to work extra hard to make ends meet, instilling in their children the values of hard work, thrift, and family unity. For Doris, these lessons would become lifelong traits, ones that defined her strength and perseverance.

Nine-year-old Doris was likely attending school, where she would have been introduced to a world of new ideas, friendships, and experiences. Schools in Ottawa, like in many parts of Canada, were predominantly Christian, so Doris's Jewish heritage may have set her apart from her classmates at times. But she would have learned how to navigate this balance, carrying her traditions with pride while also adapting to the broader Canadian culture around her. Doris's parents likely encouraged her to stay close to the Jewish community, where her family would celebrate holidays, gather for community events, and share the stories and customs that defined their identity.

At home, Doris would have been a big sister to Raymond and Greta, and her role as the eldest continued to grow. I imagine her leading the way in games, perhaps showing Raymond how to read or helping Greta with her shoes. Their parents would have relied on Doris to be responsible, encouraging her to set a good example for her siblings.

It's easy to picture her teaching them songs or telling them stories—moments that would form the foundation of their sibling bond for years to come.

Life in Ottawa in 1931 for Doris Kizell was a blend of challenges and cherished moments, each shaping her character in unique ways. She grew up surrounded by the values of her family's Jewish faith and the experiences of the larger world around her—a city filled with opportunity but marked by the hardships of the Depression. These years, although challenging, would shape Doris into a resilient young woman, connected to her family, her faith, and the broader history unfolding around her.

DORIS'S MARRIAGE TO Harry Berofe marks a significant chapter in her life. Like her, Harry was Jewish, which would have allowed the couple to share a deep connection rooted in their faith, values, and cultural heritage. This bond would have provided them with a strong foundation, especially in a time when Jewish families faced unique challenges and felt a shared responsibility to uphold and pass down their traditions.

The Jewish communities in Canada, including those in Ottawa, were close-knit, and marriage within the community was highly valued, helping to preserve traditions and religious practices. Doris and Harry's shared heritage would have strengthened their family's connection to the Jewish faith and community, ensuring that they could celebrate their customs and support each other in times of need. Together, they would have observed the High Holy Days, Shabbat, and other Jewish festivals, building a home where their heritage and identity were celebrated and passed on.

For Doris, marrying Harry meant building on the family legacy she grew up with and establishing a household that upheld the traditions she had always known. As a married woman, Doris likely stepped into a new role within the Jewish community, participating in community events, charity efforts, and gatherings that served as the heart of Jewish life. Ottawa's Jewish community would have offered them a familiar, supportive network where they could celebrate milestones, navigate challenges, and raise their family.

Marriage to Harry would bring new joys and responsibilities, giving Doris a partner with whom she could build a future, one that honored their shared past and looked forward with hope. Together, Doris and Harry Berofe would create a legacy of their own, one that wove together the threads of their heritage with their dreams for the future. Whether through stories, holiday gatherings, or simple daily rituals, they would keep alive the history and values of their ancestors, ensuring that the love and resilience that defined their heritage would carry forward into the next generation.

IN 1957, AT 35 YEARS old, Doris was living through a remarkable period in history. The launch of the Sputnik satellite on October 4, 1957, was a groundbreaking moment, igniting the Space Race and filling the world with both excitement and a sense of uncertainty. For someone like Doris, this new age of technology and exploration would have been awe-inspiring, a clear sign that the world was rapidly changing and moving toward an era of unprecedented scientific discovery.

Living in Canada, Doris would have watched these global events unfold with a unique perspective, perhaps hearing about them on the radio or reading about them in newspapers. The world was changing in ways her parents likely couldn't have imagined, and it must have been fascinating, if a bit surreal, to witness these advancements that were literally out of this world.

At this stage in her life, Doris was likely well-established in her marriage with Harry and may have had children of her own. If she did, they would be growing up in a time where science and technology were reshaping everyday life, from television sets in homes to the concept of space exploration. As a mother, Doris would have shared these exciting developments with her children, sparking curiosity and encouraging them to embrace the wonders of the future while staying connected to the values and traditions of the past.

The launch of Sputnik would have also brought with it a heightened awareness of the political tensions between the United States and the Soviet Union, an underlying anxiety of the Cold War era. Families everywhere felt the impact of this tense atmosphere, with the looming possibility of conflict casting a shadow over the excitement of technological progress. For Doris, who had grown up in a world shaped by the challenges of war and economic hardship, this new form of uncertainty would have been both familiar and unsettling.

This era of Doris's life represents a powerful blend of tradition and progress. On one hand, she was rooted in the rich heritage of her Jewish faith and culture, and on the other, she was living in a world that seemed to be rushing toward the future at an astonishing pace. Doris's life, shaped by the values her family instilled in her and her experiences growing up in Ottawa, provided her with the resilience and adaptability to navigate these changing times, both for herself and her family.

AT 47, DORIS FACED a deep and personal loss with the passing of her father, Archibald, on August 5, 1969, in Kingston, Ontario.

Losing a parent at any age is profound, but for Doris, her father's death likely brought a flood of memories and reflections. Archibald had been there through all the pivotal moments of her life—her childhood, her marriage to Harry, the births of her children—and his absence would have left a noticeable gap in the family.

The late 1960s was a period of social upheaval and change, and amidst these cultural shifts, Doris found herself confronting the personal sorrow of saying goodbye to her father. Archibald's passing would have naturally been a time for the Kizell family to come together, to reminisce about the past, and to honor his legacy. For Doris, it might have also stirred her commitment to family heritage, making her keenly aware of the importance of preserving stories and traditions for future generations.

If Doris had children, she would likely have shared stories about their grandfather, giving them a sense of connection to the family history and the values Archibald instilled in her. She would have remembered him as a steady presence during her formative years, guiding her and her siblings through life in Ottawa. Now, as an adult herself, she may have reflected on how her father's teachings influenced the woman she had become, and the ways his values had shaped her own family.

The family might have traveled to Kingston to honor Archibald's life, gathering around to mourn, celebrate, and remember. It was customary in Jewish tradition to observe shiva, a week-long period of mourning, which Doris and her family would likely have respected, coming together to share stories, support one another, and find solace in their faith. This time would allow Doris to connect deeply with her siblings, reminiscing about the family's journey, their childhood memories, and the legacy their father left behind.

For Doris, the loss of her father would mark a turning point—a moment to not only grieve but to reflect on the strength and resilience that Archibald had passed down to her. This would have become a period of introspection and reaffirmation of family ties, ensuring that Archibald's memory and the values he represented continued to be a living part of her family's story.

AT 65, DORIS EXPERIENCED the loss of her brother Aaron in 1987, an event that would have marked another emotional chapter in her life. Losing a sibling is uniquely painful; Aaron had been a constant presence from her earliest days, sharing her family history, childhood memories, and countless life moments. They had likely navigated the challenges and triumphs of life together, supporting each other through the highs and lows.

By this time, Doris may have been a grandmother herself, a matriarch in her own right, with children and grandchildren who looked to her for guidance and family stories. Aaron's passing would have been a moment of reflection, one that highlighted the importance of family bonds and the need to honor the legacies of those who came before. Doris would have felt a deep responsibility to keep Aaron's memory alive within the family, sharing stories of their shared childhood in Ottawa, his unique personality, and the bond that held them together over the years.

As the family gathered to pay their respects, Doris would likely have found comfort in the presence of her loved ones, each person connected to Aaron in different ways. The funeral, held in Kingston where Aaron had lived, would have offered a chance for family and friends to remember his life, his contributions, and his place within the family. For Doris, this loss may have underscored the preciousness of life and the importance of preserving family history for future generations.

In the years that followed, Doris would keep Aaron's memory alive through stories, memories, and shared traditions, ensuring that his spirit remained a vibrant part of their family heritage. His passing reminded her of the legacy they both carried, a testament to the values their parents had instilled and the rich history they had both lived. As Doris moved forward, she would have continued to cherish her family's shared history, determined to keep their stories alive for the generations to come.

IN 1995, AT THE AGE of 73, Doris was witnessing significant political changes in Canada, particularly as Quebec held a referendum on independence. The intense debate surrounding Quebec's potential separation from Canada was a hot topic, filled with emotions and implications for the entire nation. As a lifelong Canadian and member of a family deeply rooted in the country's history, Doris would have felt the weight of these events.

The referendum, which ultimately resulted in a narrow rejection of independence, brought to the forefront discussions about national identity, unity, and the multicultural fabric of Canada. For Doris, this moment in history might have sparked reflections on her own family's journey, particularly as Jewish immigrants and their contributions to Canadian society. Living in Ottawa, she would have been aware of the diverse cultures and communities that comprised the nation and the importance of inclusivity and understanding in maintaining a cohesive society.

During this time, Doris may have engaged in conversations with family and friends about the implications of the referendum. As a woman with a rich background in genealogy and family history, she likely understood the importance of legacy and belonging. Discussions at family gatherings could have centered around the meanings of citizenship, heritage, and the bonds that tie individuals to their communities and their country.

Doris would have been an active participant in these conversations, sharing her perspective shaped by her experiences, her family's history, and her love for Canada. As someone who had seen the world change significantly throughout her lifetime—from the Great Depression to the space race and beyond—she would have had a unique vantage point on how the nation had evolved and adapted over the years.

The rejection of Quebec's independence may have also prompted Doris to think about her own family's place within the broader context of Canadian history. With her deep appreciation for genealogy, she would have understood that the story of Canada was not just about politics but also about the myriad personal stories that contributed to its rich tapestry. As she reflected on her heritage, Doris would have felt a renewed commitment to preserving her family's history and sharing it with her children and grandchildren, ensuring that they understood the significance of their roots in an ever-changing world.

DORIS KIZELL PASSED away on January 4, 1996, in Kingston, Ontario, at the age of 74, leaving behind a legacy of resilience, love, and a profound connection to her family and heritage. Her death marked the end of a remarkable journey, one that spanned significant historical moments and personal milestones.

In her final years, Doris had likely continued to engage with her family, sharing stories of their ancestors and encouraging her children and grandchildren to appreciate their Jewish heritage. She would have been a source of wisdom and warmth, embodying the values of tradition, community, and perseverance that defined her life. Her love for genealogy, coupled with her experiences, allowed her to instill a sense of identity and belonging in her family.

After her passing, Doris was laid to rest in Beth Israel Cemetery in Kingston, Ontario, a final resting place that reflected her Jewish faith and the community she cherished. The cemetery, a serene and respectful space, would serve as a poignant reminder of her life and the impact she had on those who loved her. Family members would have gathered to mourn her loss, celebrating her life and sharing memories of the moments they had shared together.

In the days and weeks that followed her death, her family would likely have honored her memory by recalling the stories she had told and the lessons she had imparted. They might have revisited family traditions, gathering for Shabbat dinners and Jewish holidays, ensuring that her spirit lived on in the rituals she held dear. The legacy Doris created would be carried forward, as her descendants remembered her not just as a mother, sister, and aunt, but as a keeper of their family's history.

Doris's life, filled with rich experiences and a deep commitment to her roots, would continue to inspire her family for generations. Her burial in Beth Israel Cemetery would symbolize not only her final resting place but also her enduring connection to her Jewish heritage and the love that bound her family together. As her descendants visit her grave, they would be reminded of her unwavering strength, the importance of family, and the beauty of preserving their shared history.

Harry Berofe[2]

H arry was born on June 15, 1916.

Harry Berofe's life, shaped by his Lithuanian Jewish heritage, is a story reflective of many Jewish immigrants of his time who sought new opportunities in Canada. While it's uncertain exactly where Harry was born, his background is rooted in the vibrant and often tumultuous history of Lithuanian Jews.

Lithuanian Jewish Heritage

The Jewish community in Lithuania has a rich history dating back to the late Middle Ages, flourishing particularly in the 19th and early 20th centuries. During this period, Jewish culture in Lithuania was characterized by a vibrant blend of religious traditions, intellectual pursuits, and communal life. Towns often had bustling shtetls where Jewish families lived, engaged in trade, and maintained their cultural practices.

For Harry, being part of this Jewish heritage would have meant growing up with strong ties to religious traditions, including the observance of Jewish holidays, communal prayers, and the teachings of the Torah. His family may have participated in local Jewish educational institutions (cheder) where children learned about their faith and culture, instilling in them a sense of identity that was both Lithuanian and Jewish.

Immigration and Settlement

Regardless of his precise birthplace, it is likely that Harry's family faced significant challenges during his early life, particularly due to the political instability and rising antisemitism in Europe during the early

20th century. Many Jewish families, seeking safety and better opportunities, made the difficult decision to emigrate.

Harry's family may have been part of this wave of immigration to Canada during the 1920s, a time when many Eastern European Jews fled their homelands to escape persecution and poverty. Their journey to Canada would have been a significant turning point, marking the beginning of a new chapter in their lives.

Once settled in Canada, Harry and his family would have had to navigate the challenges of integrating into a new society while preserving their cultural and religious identity. This balancing act between embracing a new life in Canada and maintaining their Lithuanian Jewish roots would shape Harry's upbringing and character.

Life in Canada

As Harry grew up in Canada, the values and traditions from his Lithuanian background would continue to influence him. The close-knit Jewish community in Canada provided support and a sense of belonging, helping immigrants adjust to their new environment. Despite the uncertainties surrounding his early life, Harry would have benefited from the strength of his family and the community as they built their new lives together.

Education would have played a significant role in Harry's life. The emphasis on learning and knowledge that characterized Jewish culture likely encouraged him to pursue his studies and develop a strong work ethic. As he transitioned into adulthood, Harry would have faced the realities of the Great Depression and its impact on immigrant families. His experiences would have fostered resilience and determination, traits that would be essential in navigating the challenges of life.

Legacy of Resilience

Harry's journey from Lithuania to Canada reflects the broader narrative of Jewish immigrants who sought refuge and a better life in a new land. Even with the uncertainty of his birthplace, his Lithuanian Jewish roots were foundational to his identity, informing his values, beliefs, and family life.

Through his marriage to Doris Kizell and the life they built together, Harry would pass down the rich heritage of his ancestors to their children and grandchildren, ensuring that the stories and traditions of their Lithuanian Jewish lineage continued to thrive. His life symbolizes the resilience and adaptability of immigrant families, and the impact they had on the cultural tapestry of Canada.

AT JUST 15 YEARS OLD, Harry Berofe lived through a tumultuous period marked by the oppressive regime of Joseph Stalin, who imposed widespread terror throughout the Soviet Union, including the territories of Eastern Europe. While the exact circumstances of Harry's family during this time remain uncertain, the backdrop of political repression and fear profoundly influenced the Jewish communities in Lithuania and beyond.

The Impact of Stalin's Terror

In 1932, Stalin's policies, particularly the collectivization of agriculture and the Great Purge, led to severe consequences for various ethnic groups, including Jews. In neighboring Soviet territories, people faced arrests, executions, and widespread famine. The atmosphere of fear and paranoia created a climate where trust was scarce, and loyalty was constantly tested. For Harry and his family, this environment likely served as a reminder of the fragile nature of their safety and the importance of community solidarity.

Although Lithuania was not directly under Soviet control at the time, it was heavily influenced by the political dynamics in the region. Many Jewish families, including potentially Harry's, felt the ripple effects of Stalin's policies, which contributed to an atmosphere of uncertainty and anxiety. In 1939, as World War II loomed on the horizon, the geopolitical landscape continued to shift dramatically, with threats to Jewish communities becoming increasingly tangible.

The Role of Family and Community

In the face of such terror and instability, the importance of family and community bonds would have been paramount for Harry. Growing up in a tight-knit Jewish community would have provided a sense of security and shared identity amidst the chaos outside. Family gatherings and communal celebrations of Jewish holidays likely served as vital sources of comfort and resilience, allowing Harry to maintain a connection to his heritage while navigating the complexities of adolescence.

As a teenager, Harry would have been influenced by the experiences of older generations who had witnessed the hardships of earlier conflicts and persecutions. Stories of resilience and survival passed down through his family would have instilled in him a deep appreciation for his roots and the struggles of his ancestors. These teachings might have encouraged him to take pride in his identity and remain hopeful for the future, despite the challenges he faced.

Aspirations and Challenges

At 15, Harry would have been on the cusp of adulthood, grappling with the aspirations and challenges of young life. The uncertain political climate would have made the pursuit of education and personal goals fraught with complications. Still, he would have been determined to carve out a path for himself, perhaps focusing on the importance of education and community involvement as ways to contribute to his family and society.

The Jewish emphasis on education might have pushed Harry to excel in his studies, fostering a desire for self-improvement and understanding. As he navigated the complexities of his teenage years, he may have found solace in the arts, literature, or communal activities that resonated with his cultural identity. The interplay between his Lithuanian heritage and Canadian influences would have shaped his worldview, preparing him for the future challenges he would inevitably face.

The Precarious Nature of Life

As the years progressed and the world moved toward the brink of World War II, Harry would have remained acutely aware of the precarious nature of life as a Jewish person in an increasingly hostile environment. The lessons learned during his formative years—resilience, community strength, and the importance of heritage—would guide him as he transitioned into adulthood. His experiences during Stalin's reign would become part of his narrative, informing his perspective on the world and his commitment to protecting his family and community.

As he approached adulthood, the values instilled in him by his family and community would become the foundation of his future endeavors, shaping the life he would build alongside his future wife, Doris Kizell. Harry's journey as a Lithuanian Jew navigating the complexities of the early 20th century laid the groundwork for the legacy he would pass down to his children and grandchildren, reinforcing the importance of remembering one's roots amidst the trials of life.

IN 1957, AS THE WORLD watched the dawn of the Space Age, Harry Berofe was 40 years old. The launch of the Sputnik satellite by the Soviet Union on October 4, 1957, marked a pivotal moment in history, not just for science and technology, but also for the geopolitical landscape. This event signaled the beginning of the Space Race between the United States and the Soviet Union, a competition that would have profound implications for international relations and advancements in technology.

The Significance of Sputnik

For Harry, the launch of Sputnik represented more than just a scientific achievement; it was emblematic of the rapid advancements being made in a world that was evolving at an unprecedented pace. Living in Canada during this time, he would have been aware of the excitement and apprehension surrounding space exploration. The prospect of humans traveling into space was awe-inspiring, yet it also highlighted the technological prowess of the Soviet Union, reminding the Western world of the ongoing tensions of the Cold War.

As a father and a member of a Jewish community that had experienced its share of struggles and triumphs, Harry might have viewed the advancements in science and technology as a beacon of hope. The ability to send a satellite into orbit represented human ingenuity and the potential for progress, which resonated deeply with the values he held dear. This event likely sparked conversations within his family and community about the future and the importance of education and innovation.

Raising a Family in a Changing World

By this time, Harry and Doris were raising their family in Kingston, Ontario, and their home would have been influenced by the cultural shifts occurring around them. The late 1950s brought about a wave of optimism and progress, and Harry would have been keen on ensuring that his children understood the significance of education and the opportunities available to them in this changing world.

As a parent, Harry might have encouraged his children to pursue their interests, whether in academics, the arts, or sciences. The excitement of the Space Age would likely have been a source of inspiration for family discussions, fostering an environment where curiosity and a desire for knowledge were cherished. The family would have felt a sense of pride in belonging to a community that had overcome adversity and contributed to the fabric of Canadian society.

A Reflection on Heritage

During this period, Harry's Lithuanian Jewish heritage would have remained an integral part of his identity. The contrasting backdrop of space exploration and the ongoing struggle for equality and recognition faced by Jewish communities worldwide would have shaped his worldview. He may have reflected on the resilience of his ancestors, who had endured hardships in their homeland, and considered how far they had come in a new land that offered more freedom and opportunity.

With the Cold War backdrop of ideological conflict and the constant reminders of historical persecution, Harry would have likely instilled in his children the importance of understanding their roots and the value of standing up against injustice. His experiences, coupled with the societal changes around him, would have informed his views on community engagement and social responsibility.

Embracing Change

As the 1960s approached, Harry would have been both excited and apprehensive about the changes that lay ahead. The world was on the brink of significant transformation, with the civil rights movement gaining momentum, advancements in technology reshaping everyday life, and cultural revolutions stirring up a desire for equality and expression.

For Harry, who had witnessed both the struggles of his youth and the triumphs of his community, this was a time to reflect on the importance of progress—both in the scientific realm and in social justice. The launch of Sputnik not only represented technological advancement but also echoed the broader aspirations of humanity to reach for the stars, pushing the boundaries of what was possible.

Harry's story is one of resilience, hope, and the ongoing journey of a family deeply rooted in their heritage while navigating the complexities of an ever-changing world. As he continued to embrace the challenges and opportunities of the 1960s, Harry would carry with him the lessons learned from both his past and the advancements of his time, shaping the legacy he would pass on to future generations.

IN 1982, AT THE AGE of 65, Harry Berofe witnessed the introduction of audio CDs (compact discs) to the market. This technological innovation revolutionized the way music was consumed, marking a significant shift from vinyl records and cassette tapes to a new digital format that promised superior sound quality and convenience.

The Arrival of CDs

For Harry, the emergence of audio CDs symbolized the rapid pace of technological advancement that had characterized his lifetime. This shift not only transformed the music industry but also reflected broader changes in society. The compact disc offered a new way to experience music, allowing for greater accessibility and portability. As someone who had lived through the early days of recorded sound, from the crackling of vinyl to the hiss of cassette tapes, Harry likely found the clarity and durability of CDs remarkable.

A New Way to Experience Music

Music had always held a special place in Harry's life. Growing up in a Jewish household, he would have been familiar with traditional melodies and folk songs that connected him to his heritage. As an adult, he may have enjoyed a diverse range of musical styles, from classical to popular music. With the introduction of CDs, Harry would have likely embraced this new format, appreciating the ease with which he could curate his music collection.

Family gatherings may have featured the sounds of his favorite artists playing on the CD player, bringing a sense of joy and nostalgia. The ability to create playlists and enjoy music without the interruptions that came with older formats would have resonated with Harry, making it easier to share his love of music with his children and grandchildren.

The Changing Landscape of Technology

As he embraced this new technology, Harry would have been acutely aware of the significant changes occurring in the world around him. The rise of digital technology and the increasing influence of computers in everyday life were reshaping society, impacting everything from communication to entertainment. Harry, who had navigated significant historical events throughout his life, would have seen this shift as part of a broader narrative of progress.

At 65, Harry might have reflected on how far the world had come since his youth, particularly in terms of innovation and accessibility. The audio CD era represented not only a leap forward in technology but also a new chapter in how families experienced music together, fostering connection and creating memories through shared musical moments.

Legacy and Family Connections

With a family that cherished its Jewish roots and celebrated cultural traditions, the introduction of CDs could have also served as a bridge between generations. Harry might have taken joy in sharing music from his own youth, introducing his children and grandchildren to the sounds that shaped his early life while also exploring contemporary artists together. The compact disc would have been a tool for storytelling, allowing him to weave personal narratives into the fabric of his family's musical heritage.

Harry's appreciation for the arts, whether through music or other forms, would have been a significant aspect of his legacy. He likely encouraged his family to embrace creativity, instilling in them the value of artistic expression as a means of understanding the world and connecting with one another. The CDs they listened to together would not only provide entertainment but also serve as reminders of family gatherings, celebrations, and shared experiences.

Reflecting on a Life of Change

As the 1980s unfolded, Harry, now a seasoned elder, would have seen the world continue to change at a rapid pace. The advent of CDs was just one example of how technology was transforming everyday life, and he would have approached these changes with a blend of curiosity and caution. He likely remained an avid learner, keeping up with new developments and adapting to the shifting cultural landscape.

Harry's journey through the decades, from his childhood in a politically tumultuous Europe to his role as a father and grandfather in a new land, reflects a life rich with experiences. As he navigated the complexities of modern life, the introduction of audio CDs represented yet another chapter in his ongoing story—a testament to the resilience of his family and the enduring power of music to bring people together across generations.

IN JANUARY 1996, HARRY Berofe faced one of the most challenging moments of his life at the age of 79: the passing of his beloved wife, Doris. She died on January 4 in Kingston, Ontario, leaving a profound void in his life and in the hearts of their family and friends.

A Life Together

Doris and Harry had built a life filled with love, family, and shared experiences. Their marriage was a partnership that had weathered the storms of life, from the challenges of raising children to the joys of celebrating milestones together. As Jewish immigrants, they had also embraced their heritage, instilling a sense of identity and tradition in their family. Doris's warmth and devotion had been a cornerstone of their family life, providing not just emotional support but also creating a nurturing environment for their children and grandchildren.

With Doris's passing, Harry lost not just a spouse but also his closest companion and confidante. The years they spent together had forged a bond that was deep and meaningful. He would have reflected on the countless memories they shared: family dinners filled with laughter, quiet evenings spent listening to music, and their shared dreams and aspirations.

Grief and Reflection

The grief Harry experienced after Doris's death was undoubtedly overwhelming. As he navigated this profound loss, he might have found solace in reminiscing about their life together, recalling Doris's laughter, her kindness, and the way she brought joy to those around her. The songs they had shared, possibly on those newly cherished CDs, might have become bittersweet reminders of their journey together.

At this stage in his life, Harry would have drawn strength from his family, who likely rallied around him during this difficult time. The legacy of love that Doris had created within the family would have provided a support network, reminding Harry that he was not alone in his sorrow. Their children and grandchildren would have been a source of comfort, helping him to honor Doris's memory and ensuring that her spirit lived on in the stories they shared.

The Importance of Legacy

Doris's passing may have prompted Harry to reflect deeply on their shared legacy. He might have felt a renewed sense of responsibility to preserve their family history and ensure that the stories of their ancestors were passed down to future generations. This could have included documenting their experiences as immigrants, the traditions they upheld, and the values they instilled in their children.

Harry may have taken it upon himself to create a family archive, collecting photographs, letters, and other memorabilia that celebrated Doris's life and their journey together. By doing so, he would have honored her memory while also reinforcing the importance of family history and connection—a passion that had always been a significant part of his life.

Facing the Future

Despite the profound loss, Harry would have understood that life must continue. As he navigated the path of grief, he might have sought ways to celebrate Doris's life rather than solely mourning her absence. This could have included honoring her favorite traditions, perhaps hosting family gatherings that mirrored the celebrations they once enjoyed together.

As the years rolled on, Harry would have learned to carry Doris's memory with him, integrating it into his daily life. He might have visited her grave at Beth Israel Cemetery in Kingston, reflecting on their shared moments and drawing strength from the love that would forever bind them.

A Testament to Love

Harry's life after Doris's passing would have been a testament to the enduring power of love and memory. Though he faced the challenges of aging without his partner by his side, he would have remained committed to living a life that honored the values they both cherished.

In the days ahead, he would continue to share stories with family, celebrate the milestones of his children and grandchildren, and perhaps even reflect on the lessons he had learned from Doris. He would strive to find joy in the little things—a familiar song on the radio, a family gathering, or a quiet moment in nature—each serving as a reminder of the love they had shared.

Harry Berofe's journey, shaped by both triumphs and tribulations, illustrated the resilience of the human spirit. Through his memories of Doris and the love they had cultivated together, he would carry forward a legacy that transcended time, ensuring that her spirit lived on in the hearts of those they had touched.

AT THE AGE OF 84, HARRY Berofe witnessed one of the most harrowing events in modern history: the terrorist attacks on September 11, 2001. As the news broke of planes crashing into the World Trade Center in New York City and the Pentagon in Washington, D.C., Harry, like millions around the world, was drawn into a state of shock and disbelief.

Reflecting on a World Changed

Having lived through significant historical events—from the rise of totalitarian regimes in Europe to the civil rights movements and the advent of new technologies—Harry had seen the world transform in profound ways. However, the brutality and suddenness of the 9/11 attacks marked a pivotal moment in history that would change not only the United States but the entire world.

For Harry, the attacks likely stirred memories of his own experiences with loss and terror during his early years in Europe. He would have been reminded of the struggles faced by Jewish communities during World War II and the importance of solidarity in the face of adversity. These reflections might have deepened his empathy for the victims and their families, as well as the global ramifications of such violence.

A Nation in Mourning

In the aftermath of the attacks, Harry would have watched as the nation mourned and responded to the tragedy. The outpouring of grief and unity among the American people might have resonated with him, highlighting the enduring human spirit in times of crisis. He would have seen people coming together to support one another, reminiscent of the solidarity shown in previous decades during difficult times.

Harry might have also engaged in conversations with family and friends about the significance of the events unfolding around them. As an elder who had lived through various historical moments, he would have offered a unique perspective on resilience, hope, and the need for compassion in a fractured world. Sharing his insights would have helped younger generations process their feelings about the attacks and the subsequent changes in global politics.

The Aftermath and Its Impact

As the United States entered into a period of heightened security and military action, Harry would have felt the implications of these changes ripple through society. The fear and uncertainty that followed 9/11 reshaped the landscape of global relations and domestic policies, affecting countless lives. Harry, having experienced the effects of war and displacement in his youth, may have had complex feelings about the measures taken in the name of security.

He would have been concerned about the rise of xenophobia and prejudice that emerged in the wake of the attacks. Harry's own Jewish heritage likely made him acutely aware of the dangers of scapegoating and the importance of standing up against hate. He may have felt a sense of duty to speak out against intolerance, advocating for understanding and compassion among people of all backgrounds.

Legacy and Reflection

At 84, Harry remained committed to preserving the lessons of history, imparting wisdom to his children and grandchildren about the value of peace, tolerance, and the need for vigilance against hatred. He might have used this time to reflect on his own life experiences and how they paralleled the unfolding events in the world around him.

In family gatherings, he could have shared stories from his past, illustrating the importance of resilience and community in overcoming challenges. His legacy of strength and perseverance would have become even more crucial in the context of the changing world, serving as a reminder of the power of love and unity in the face of adversity.

Navigating a New Reality

As Harry continued to navigate life in a post-9/11 world, he might have found solace in small moments—family dinners, the laughter of grandchildren, and the shared love of music. He would have taken comfort in knowing that, despite the turmoil in the world, his family remained a source of strength and joy.

The tragic events of September 11, 2001, marked a turning point not just for Harry but for an entire generation. For him, it was a time to reflect on the fragility of life, the importance of community, and the enduring power of hope. As he moved forward, he would remain dedicated to honoring the memories of those lost in the attacks while continuing to embrace the values of love, empathy, and resilience that had guided him throughout his life.

ON JUNE 1, 2008, HARRY Berofe passed away in Kingston, Ontario, at the age of 91, leaving behind a rich legacy of love, resilience, and a commitment to family and community. His death marked the end of an era, one that had witnessed incredible transformations in society, technology, and culture.

A Life Well-Lived

Harry's life spanned nearly a century, during which he experienced the joys and sorrows that come with the human experience. He had navigated through tumultuous times—world wars, personal loss, and the challenges of immigration—yet he always remained steadfast in his values. Family was at the center of his life, and his dedication to nurturing those relationships was evident in everything he did.

As he entered his later years, Harry often reflected on the memories that defined him: his marriage to Doris, the upbringing of their children, and the shared moments that brought them closer. He cherished family gatherings, where laughter filled the air, and stories of the past were recounted with love and warmth. These moments were not just about reminiscing but were vital to keeping the family history alive.

The Final Years

In the years leading up to his passing, Harry may have faced health challenges typical of advancing age. However, his spirit remained unbroken. He was known for his ability to find joy in simple pleasures—a walk in the park, a good book, or the company of loved ones. Despite the physical limitations that came with age, he maintained an active interest in the world around him, staying informed and engaged with current events.

Harry's wisdom and experience made him a cherished figure in the family. His children and grandchildren likely sought his guidance and perspective on various matters, drawing on the depth of his knowledge and the life lessons he had accumulated over the years. He remained a source of strength and stability, a comforting presence in their lives.

Legacy of Love

On the day of his passing, those who knew him would have gathered to celebrate his life and to reflect on the profound impact he had made. Family members would share anecdotes that highlighted Harry's kindness, generosity, and unwavering spirit. The stories would flow freely, painting a vivid picture of a man who lived with integrity and compassion.

Harry's burial in Beth Israel Cemetery in Kingston, Ontario, marked a poignant conclusion to his life. In that serene setting, his loved ones would have found solace, knowing he was laid to rest in a place that held significance for his family. As they visited his grave, they would continue to honor his memory, sharing stories and traditions that kept his spirit alive in their hearts.

Continuing the Legacy

In the years that followed Harry's passing, his family would likely strive to uphold the values he instilled in them: love, empathy, and a deep appreciation for their heritage. Doris and Harry's story, woven together through decades of shared experiences, would continue to resonate, inspiring the next generations to cherish their roots and the history that shaped their identities.

As a family, they might have created a tradition of gathering at the cemetery on significant dates, celebrating birthdays, anniversaries, or simply to reminisce about Harry's life. These gatherings would serve as a reminder of the importance of family ties and the stories that bind them together.

Reflection and Remembrance

In the quiet moments of reflection, Harry's family would remember him not just as a father or grandfather but as a guardian of their family history. His passion for genealogy and storytelling would encourage them to delve into their own ancestry, exploring the rich tapestry of their Jewish roots and the experiences of those who came before them.

Harry Berofe's life story, marked by love and perseverance, serves as a testament to the strength of the human spirit. Even after his passing, his influence would continue to guide his family, reminding them to cherish each other, to learn from the past, and to embrace the future with hope and resilience. Through their stories and traditions, Harry's legacy would live on, echoing through generations as a reminder of the bonds that unite them.

Beryl Ruth Cowan[3]

Beryl Ruth Cowan was born on November 6, 1959, a time rich with historical significance and social change. As I reflect on the world into which she entered, I can't help but marvel at the tapestry of events and cultural shifts that would shape her life and, in turn, influence her own exploration of family history.

The World in 1959

In Canada, the late 1950s were marked by a post-war optimism that filled the air with possibilities. The nation was experiencing a baby boom, with families flourishing and new suburbs emerging to accommodate the influx of young households. It was a time when the American Dream was taking root, and families, like Beryl's, aspired to own homes, raise children, and build a future filled with promise.

This era was not just about expansion but also about connection. Families gathered around televisions for entertainment, tuning in to shows that reflected their values and aspirations. The Ed Sullivan Show introduced stars who would become legends, while sitcoms like Leave It to Beaver presented an idealized view of family life. For someone like Beryl, who would later weave together the stories of her ancestors, these moments of shared culture would serve as the backdrop to her formative years.

The Cultural Shift

The cultural landscape of the late 1950s was a melting pot of creativity and expression. Rock and roll music echoed through homes and neighborhoods, providing a soundtrack to the lives of young people discovering their voices. Icons like Elvis Presley and Chuck Berry were not just entertainers; they were catalysts for change, encouraging youth to embrace freedom and individuality.

As Beryl grew, she would witness firsthand the tension between the emerging counterculture and the traditional values of her upbringing. This dynamic would become especially poignant as she delved into her own family history, seeking to understand how her ancestors navigated their lives during tumultuous times.

A Focus on Education

During this period, education was gaining prominence, with schools beginning to emphasize science and technology as essential components of a modern curriculum. This focus on learning and advancement resonated deeply within Beryl's family, who instilled in her a love for exploration and knowledge. The value they placed on education would undoubtedly play a crucial role in shaping her curiosity about her lineage.

The Political Landscape

The backdrop of the Cold War loomed large, with international tensions rising as the United States and the Soviet Union vied for supremacy. The launch of Sputnik in 1957 marked a pivotal moment in history, igniting a space race that captivated the imagination of a generation. This era of uncertainty would influence Beryl's worldview and perhaps inspire her to seek out the stories of resilience and courage in her family's past.

Family and Heritage

Beryl's Jewish heritage provided a rich tapestry of tradition and history. As she entered the world, she was surrounded by a community that cherished its roots and emphasized the importance of family. Stories of ancestors who came before her were likely shared during family gatherings, instilling a sense of pride and connection to her lineage. This nurturing environment would shape her identity and ignite her passion for genealogy.

A Legacy of Exploration

As I think about Beryl's beginnings in that transformative year, I can see how the events of her time intertwined with the legacy of her ancestors. Born into a world full of change and opportunity, she was destined to become a seeker of stories, a weaver of her family's history. The threads of her life, woven with the fabric of the past, would inspire her to explore the lives of those who came before her, ensuring their memories would endure for generations to come.

BERYL RUTH COWAN WAS just one year old when Russian astronaut Yuri Gagarin made history by becoming the first human to orbit the Earth on April 12, 1961. This monumental event marked a significant milestone in the Space Race, showcasing humanity's ingenuity and determination to explore the unknown.

A World of Possibilities

As Beryl entered her second year of life, the world around her was buzzing with excitement over Gagarin's achievement. His successful flight symbolized not only the triumph of science and technology but also the boundless potential of human achievement. Families and communities were inspired by the notion that anything was possible if one dared to dream big.

Impact on Society

For the young families of the time, including Beryl's, this era represented hope and aspiration. Parents were motivated to foster a sense of wonder in their children, encouraging them to pursue knowledge and explore their own interests. This spirit of exploration would later become a hallmark of Beryl's journey into genealogy, as she would seek to uncover the stories and legacies of her ancestors.

A Time of Innovation

The early 1960s were a period marked by rapid advancements in technology, culture, and social norms. In addition to the excitement surrounding space exploration, new inventions were revolutionizing everyday life. From the introduction of color television to the growing popularity of household appliances, these innovations transformed how families lived, communicated, and connected with one another.

As Beryl grew, the world around her was evolving. The cultural landscape was filled with music, art, and a burgeoning sense of identity that was being shaped by the experiences of the post-war generation. This backdrop would undoubtedly influence Beryl's own perspective as she navigated her path through life.

The Seeds of Curiosity

Though she was too young to comprehend the significance of Gagarin's journey, the event would leave an indelible mark on her formative years. The idea of exploration—whether in the cosmos or within the fabric of her family's history—would resonate with her throughout her life.

As Beryl entered her early childhood, her family's stories, combined with the era's spirit of curiosity, would ignite her passion for uncovering the past. The seeds of her genealogical journey were planted in this rich tapestry of history, innovation, and cultural evolution, setting the stage for the lifelong quest that would define her legacy.

AT THE AGE OF 22, BERYL Ruth Cowan found herself living in a world that was on the brink of a technological revolution with the introduction of audio CDs in 1982. This new format promised a richer, clearer listening experience, transforming how people consumed music and other audio media.

The Digital Dawn

The arrival of audio CDs marked the beginning of the digital age, and Beryl was part of a generation witnessing the transition from analog to digital. Growing up in the late 1970s and early 1980s, she had likely enjoyed music on vinyl records and cassette tapes. Now, as CDs hit the market, the allure of a new, superior sound quality was enticing for music lovers everywhere.

As a young adult, Beryl would have been captivated by the cultural shifts occurring around her. Music was an essential part of social gatherings and personal expression, and the introduction of CDs made it easier to share and enjoy music. This new technology changed how people interacted with music; playlists could now be curated and recorded with ease, allowing for a more personalized listening experience.

Cultural Influences

The early 1980s were a vibrant time for music, marked by the rise of iconic artists and bands, from Michael Jackson and Madonna to The Police and Prince. This era's pop culture profoundly influenced Beryl and her peers, as they embraced new genres and styles that reflected the spirit of the times. The music video became a significant medium for expression, and shows like MTV played an essential role in launching the careers of many artists.

For Beryl, this was not just about entertainment; it was about connecting with her generation and understanding the narratives woven through the lyrics and rhythms. Music often serves as a bridge between generations, and as she listened to the popular hits of the day, she may have felt a sense of nostalgia for the stories of her own family that shaped her identity.

Personal Growth and Exploration

As Beryl navigated her early twenties, she was likely discovering her own interests and passions. The empowerment and freedom that accompanied the rise of new music and technology may have inspired her to explore her roots more deeply. Perhaps she began to reflect on her family's journey, seeking to understand how their stories intersected with the broader cultural shifts occurring around her.

This newfound appreciation for her heritage would have been enriched by the ability to document her family history in new and exciting ways, making connections across time and space. The ease of recording and sharing information mirrored her passion for genealogy, allowing her to compile her family's narratives with greater accessibility.

A Generational Connection

At 22, Beryl stood at the crossroads of tradition and innovation. The impact of audio CDs extended beyond just the music industry; it symbolized a shift in how people communicated and connected with one another. As she immersed herself in this evolving landscape, Beryl may have found parallels between the stories of her ancestors and the modern experiences unfolding around her.

In this exciting moment, Beryl was not only a witness to technological advancements but also an active participant in a cultural movement that emphasized exploration, self-expression, and connection.

BERYL RUTH COWAN PASSED away at the age of 62 on April 17, 2022, in Kingston, Ontario. She is buried in Beth Israel Cemetery, a place that reflects her deep connection to her roots and community.

A Life Remembered

Beryl's life was rich with experiences that resonated with those who knew her. She carried with her a wealth of stories, shaped by the moments she shared with family and friends. Though she may not have been known for any specific pursuits, the impact she had on the lives of her loved ones was profound.

Family Connections

Throughout her life, Beryl likely found joy in the simple pleasures of family gatherings, celebrations, and shared memories. Her warmth and kindness created an atmosphere of love that drew people together, making her home a welcoming space for all. The laughter and stories exchanged during these times would have created lasting impressions, enriching the bonds between family members.

A Legacy of Love

Beryl's legacy lives on in the hearts of those she touched. Her caring nature and genuine spirit will be remembered by family and friends as they carry forward the values she instilled in them. The lessons learned from her life—compassion, resilience, and the importance of cherishing moments with loved ones—will continue to guide them in their own journeys.

As she rests in Beth Israel Cemetery, Beryl's spirit remains a vital part of her family's narrative. Her life was a testament to the beauty of connection and the significance of nurturing relationships that endure through time. While her physical presence may be gone, the love and memories she created will forever be cherished by those who knew her.

Alfred Joel Fisher[4]

———

Alfred Joel Fisher was born on June 30, 1942, in Boston, Massachusetts, during a period that was marked by significant global and domestic events. His early years were influenced by the aftermath of World War II, the Jewish experience in America, and the burgeoning cultural changes of the 1960s.

The World in 1942

In 1942, the world was engulfed in World War II. The United States had entered the war following the attack on Pearl Harbor in December 1941, and the conflict was profoundly affecting life in America. The country was mobilizing for war, and many citizens were directly involved in supporting the war effort, whether through military service or working in factories that produced munitions and supplies.

For Jewish families, the war's impact was particularly poignant. The Holocaust was unfolding in Europe, with millions of Jews facing persecution and death. In this context, the Jewish community in America was both aware of the atrocities happening overseas and engaged in efforts to support refugees and raise awareness about the plight of European Jews.

Boston in the 1940s

Boston, with its rich history and vibrant cultural scene, provided a unique backdrop for Alfred's early life. The city was known for its significant Jewish population, which had been established through waves of immigration. Many Jewish families in Boston were working-class, and they contributed to the city's diverse cultural landscape.

As Alfred was born into this environment, he likely experienced the traditions and values that shaped Jewish life in America. Jewish communities in Boston engaged in various social and religious activities, fostering a sense of identity and solidarity during a challenging time.

The Post-War Era

As Alfred grew up, the post-war era ushered in a period of prosperity and change. The late 1940s and 1950s saw significant economic growth in the United States, leading to an expansion of the middle class. Many families moved to suburban areas, and the baby boom began, significantly influencing American society.

For Jewish families, this era also brought a renewed emphasis on education and cultural assimilation. Alfred's upbringing would have been marked by a commitment to education and the values of hard work, which were common among Jewish families seeking to integrate into American society while preserving their heritage.

The Cultural Shifts of the 1960s

By the time Alfred reached adolescence, the cultural landscape was shifting dramatically. The 1960s were characterized by social upheaval, civil rights movements, and the counterculture revolution. Young people began to challenge traditional norms and express themselves in new ways, influenced by music, art, and social movements.

Alfred would have witnessed these changes during his formative years, and they likely influenced his worldview and values. The experiences of growing up in a Jewish household amidst these societal shifts may have instilled in him a sense of identity that combined both cultural pride and a commitment to social justice.

Conclusion

Alfred Joel Fisher's life began during a tumultuous time in history, yet it was also a period of resilience and transformation. His experiences as a Jewish child in Boston during the early 1940s would have shaped his understanding of identity, community, and the importance of standing up against injustice. As he grew older, he carried with him the lessons of his upbringing and the legacy of those who came before him, navigating a world that was constantly evolving while holding fast to his heritage.

ALFRED JOEL FISHER was just 7 years old when the Korean War began on June 25, 1950. This conflict marked a significant moment in history, and although he was still a child, the war would leave an indelible impact on the world around him and, by extension, his formative years.

The Korean War and Its Context

The Korean War was a pivotal event that saw North Korea, supported by the Soviet Union and China, invade South Korea, leading to a military response from the United Nations, primarily driven by the United States. The war lasted until 1953, resulting in a divided Korea that still endures to this day. As a young boy in Boston during this time, Alfred was likely exposed to the anxiety and fear that permeated American society. The conflict, coupled with the ongoing tensions of the Cold War, was a reminder of the precariousness of peace and the realities of global politics.

Childhood During Turbulent Times

Growing up in a Jewish family, Alfred's childhood was colored by the memories of World War II and the Holocaust, which were still fresh in the minds of many. His parents, having experienced the traumas of the past, likely shared stories that instilled a strong sense of identity and resilience within him. In the face of global conflict, families were often reminded of the importance of community and support, values that would shape Alfred's character and creative spirit.

As a child, Alfred may have found solace in the arts, drawing inspiration from the rich cultural environment of Boston. The city was a hub for creativity and intellectual pursuits, where music, literature, and the arts flourished. With his natural talents, he may have gravitated toward music and writing as outlets for expression during a time of uncertainty, helping him process the world around him.

Impact on Future Generations

The Korean War, along with the global tensions of the 1950s, would ultimately influence the course of history and the outlook of future generations, including Alfred. As he grew older, he would develop a keen awareness of the complexities of human experience, reflecting these themes in his writing and music. The struggles of the past and present shaped his perspective, inspiring him to create works that resonated with the human condition.

In many ways, Alfred's early exposure to conflict and resilience became a backdrop for his later endeavors as an artist and educator. He would go on to instill in his students not just a love for music and literature but also an understanding of the importance of addressing societal issues through creative expression.

Conclusion

At 7 years old, as the Korean War erupted, Alfred Joel Fisher was growing up in a world marked by conflict, resilience, and the pursuit of artistic expression. These formative years, shaped by the realities of global events and the warmth of his community, laid the foundation for a life dedicated to creativity, teaching, and a profound appreciation for the natural world. His experiences during this turbulent time would undoubtedly influence his outlook on life, art, and the connections between individuals and their shared histories.

———————————

ALFRED JOEL FISHER was just 20 years old when President John F. Kennedy was assassinated on November 22, 1963. This tragic event sent shockwaves across the United States and the world, deeply impacting the collective consciousness of a generation that had come of age during a time of both hope and upheaval.

A Defining Moment in History

Kennedy's assassination marked a pivotal moment in American history. It symbolized the abrupt end of a promising era characterized by progressive ideals and youthful optimism. For Alfred, who was a young adult navigating his path in the world, this event was not merely a political upheaval but a personal one, too. The shock and disbelief that followed Kennedy's death were palpable, shaping how many viewed their nation and its leadership.

As a student and budding artist, Alfred was likely influenced by the cultural and political climate of the time. The 1960s were rife with social change—civil rights movements, anti-war protests, and a growing counterculture. These currents would have resonated deeply with Alfred as he explored his identity and voice as a writer and composer. He may have found himself grappling with the weight of these events, channeling his feelings of loss, anger, and confusion into his art.

The Influence of the 1960s

The assassination brought about a period of intense reflection and activism among young people. The world Alfred inhabited was increasingly characterized by a desire for change and a questioning of the status quo. This environment was conducive to creativity, inspiring many artists to address pressing societal issues in their work. Alfred, with his passion for music and literature, likely felt a compulsion to engage with the world around him, expressing the hopes and fears of a generation through his compositions and poetry.

In the aftermath of Kennedy's death, the atmosphere of mourning was tangible, yet so too was the sense of urgency for reform and progress. Many young Americans became politically active, advocating for civil rights and opposing the Vietnam War. This era of upheaval likely shaped Alfred's worldview, influencing the themes he explored in his writing and compositions—questions of identity, morality, and the complexities of the human experience.

A Lasting Legacy

As Alfred continued his journey in the arts, the impact of Kennedy's assassination and the subsequent social movements would inform his work and teaching philosophy. He understood the power of art to reflect and challenge societal norms, and he would instill this understanding in his students, encouraging them to use their voices and creativity to address the world's complexities.

The legacy of that fateful day in November 1963 lingered in the collective memory, reminding generations to come of the fragility of life and the importance of hope and resilience in the face of adversity. For Alfred, who was beginning to carve out his place in a rapidly changing world, this moment would serve as a catalyst for reflection and action in both his life and career.

Conclusion

At 20 years old, Alfred Joel Fisher was not just a witness to the assassination of President Kennedy but also a participant in a larger narrative of change and introspection. The profound sorrow and uncertainty that followed this event became woven into the fabric of his generation's consciousness. As he moved forward in his artistic endeavors, he would draw upon this pivotal moment, ultimately shaping a career that was as much about personal expression as it was about connecting with the broader human experience during a time of tumult and transformation.

ALFRED JOEL FISHER became a Canadian citizen in 1974, a significant milestone that marked the beginning of a new chapter in his life. Embracing his identity as a Canadian, he immersed himself in the cultural and natural beauty of his new home, drawing inspiration from the vast landscapes that surrounded him.

A Passion for the Arts

As a writer, poet, and professor, Alfred's creative pursuits flourished in Canada. His talent as a composer and pianist was exceptional, and his music resonated with audiences far and wide. His compositions, known for their emotive depth and technical brilliance, were performed and broadcast globally, earning him recognition in the music community. Alfred's ability to blend classical traditions with contemporary influences allowed him to create a unique voice that reflected his diverse experiences.

In the classroom, Alfred inspired countless students with his passion for music and literature. His teaching career spanned several esteemed institutions, including the Department of Music at the University of Western Ontario, Acadia University, the University of Alberta, and Queen's University. His students were captivated not only by his knowledge and expertise but also by his enthusiasm for nurturing their creativity. Alfred encouraged them to explore their musical voices and cultivate their talents, fostering a love for the arts that many carried into their own careers.

Love for Nature and Adventure

Beyond his artistic endeavors, Alfred was an ardent lover of nature, finding solace and inspiration in the Canadian wilderness. The beauty of the northern landscapes, with their majestic mountains, serene lakes, and expansive forests, captivated him. He often ventured into the great outdoors, engaging in activities such as fishing and hiking that allowed him to connect deeply with the natural world.

Alfred's adventures in the Canadian north were not just recreational; they were also a source of inspiration for his creative work. The tranquility of nature infused his music with a sense of peace and reflection, while the ruggedness of the landscape mirrored the complexities of life that he explored in his writing. He understood the profound relationship between art and nature, often drawing parallels between the two in his teachings and compositions.

A Lasting Impact

Alfred's multifaceted career and deep appreciation for both the arts and the natural world left a lasting impact on those who knew him. He was more than just a professor; he was a mentor, a friend, and a guiding light for many aspiring artists. His dedication to his craft and his ability to inspire others became a hallmark of his legacy.

Through his music, writings, and teachings, Alfred Joel Fisher contributed to the rich tapestry of Canadian culture, leaving behind a treasure trove of creativity that continues to inspire future generations. His life was a testament to the power of art and nature, and his adventurous spirit exemplified the essence of exploration and expression. As he embraced his identity as a Canadian, he not only enriched his own life but also the lives of countless others who crossed his path.

———————————

ALFRED JOEL FISHER was 39 years old when audio CDs were introduced to the public in 1982, marking a revolutionary advancement in music technology. This innovation was significant not just for the music industry but also for listeners like Alfred, who cherished music as an integral part of their lives.

The Dawn of Digital Music

The introduction of audio CDs changed the way people consumed music. Gone were the days of vinyl records and cassette tapes, which often came with their own limitations in terms of sound quality and durability. CDs offered a crisp, clear sound that was unprecedented, allowing listeners to experience their favorite compositions in ways they had never imagined. For Alfred, a talented composer and musician, this technological shift opened new avenues for both creating and sharing his work.

As an educator in the Department of Music at the University of Western Ontario, Alfred embraced this change with enthusiasm. The CD format allowed for a new level of precision in the recording and playback of music, which would undoubtedly influence the teaching methods he employed in his classroom. With the ability to access high-quality recordings, students could better appreciate the nuances of various musical styles and compositions, expanding their understanding of music theory and history.

Embracing the Change

During this period, Alfred may have been particularly excited about the opportunities that CDs presented for his own compositions. The digital format not only allowed him to produce and distribute his music more widely but also reached a new generation of listeners who were beginning to embrace this innovative medium. As he experimented with different sounds and styles, the advent of CDs could have inspired him to explore the possibilities of recording technology, enabling him to push the boundaries of his artistic expression.

This era also saw a surge in the production of classical music recordings on CD, allowing Alfred's students and fellow musicians to study the works of composers both past and contemporary with greater ease. It was a transformative time for music education, and Alfred was well-positioned to harness these advancements, encouraging his students to appreciate the depth and complexity of music through this new medium.

The Cultural Impact

The introduction of audio CDs also coincided with significant cultural shifts in the 1980s. Music was becoming more accessible, and the rise of personal music collections allowed individuals to curate their listening experiences in a way that had previously been limited by the format of records or tapes. For Alfred, this meant that the audience for his music could grow exponentially. The potential for increased visibility through CD releases and radio play opened doors for both him and his students, further intertwining their artistic journeys with the evolving landscape of music consumption.

Conclusion

At 39, Alfred Joel Fisher stood at the intersection of tradition and innovation as audio CDs were introduced to the world. This technological advancement was not just a change in format but a catalyst for creativity, collaboration, and exploration within the music community. For Alfred, it represented an opportunity to connect with audiences in new ways, fostering a deeper appreciation for the art of music in all its forms. As he navigated this exciting time in the music world, he undoubtedly inspired his students to embrace the possibilities that lay ahead, shaping the future of music education and composition for years to come.

ALFRED JOEL FISHER was 58 years old when the tragic events of September 11, 2001, unfolded. The world watched in shock and disbelief as terrorist attacks struck the United States, leaving an indelible mark on the global consciousness. This catastrophic day not only reshaped geopolitics but also had profound implications for individuals like Alfred, an artist deeply connected to the cultural and emotional currents of society.

A Moment of Global Shock

On that fateful morning, as news of the attacks spread, people around the world were gripped by fear and uncertainty. For Alfred, who had spent his life teaching and creating art, the events of 9/11 may have sparked a wave of reflection and introspection. Music, as a universal language, became a powerful medium for processing the grief, anger, and confusion that followed. Artists, including Alfred, were faced with the challenge of responding to this tragedy, using their creative talents to provide comfort, solidarity, and understanding in a time of crisis.

The Role of Music in Healing

In the aftermath of 9/11, many musicians and composers turned to their art as a means of healing. The power of music to express complex emotions and to unite people became even more apparent. Alfred, with his deep appreciation for nature and human experience, likely felt compelled to address the turmoil through his work. He may have drawn upon the themes of resilience and hope, creating compositions that resonated with the collective grief of a nation.

This period also witnessed an increase in the use of music for public memorials and gatherings. Concerts and events honoring the victims became spaces for community and remembrance, allowing people to come together in solidarity. As a professor and a musician, Alfred might have encouraged his students to explore the role of music in fostering healing and connection during such difficult times, urging them to use their craft as a response to the challenges of the world.

Cultural and Social Shifts

The events of 9/11 not only affected individual artists but also led to significant cultural and social shifts. In the years that followed, the landscape of music and art was influenced by the desire for understanding and dialogue. Alfred, as an educator, may have found himself engaging in discussions about the impact of terrorism, identity, and the role of art in society. These conversations would have enriched the educational experience for his students, prompting them to consider the broader implications of their work.

The attacks also ignited a wave of patriotism and introspection across North America, affecting the themes explored in contemporary music. As artists began to grapple with questions of identity and belonging, Alfred's work likely became a reflection of the changing landscape. He may have found inspiration in the resilience of the human spirit, channeling his experiences into compositions that celebrated hope and unity in the face of adversity.

Conclusion

At 58, Alfred Joel Fisher experienced the world shifting dramatically around him due to the events of 9/11. The tragedy highlighted the profound impact that art, particularly music, could have in times of crisis. For Alfred, this period became an opportunity to engage with his students and the community, using his talents to foster understanding and connection during a time of uncertainty. As he navigated the complexities of this new reality, Alfred's artistry would not only reflect his personal journey but also resonate with the broader human experience, ultimately contributing to the ongoing dialogue about resilience, hope, and the healing power of music.

ALFRED JOEL FISHER passed away at the age of 74 on December 13, 2016, in Kingston, Ontario, leaving behind a legacy rich in artistry, education, and a deep appreciation for the natural world. His death marked the end of a remarkable life dedicated to music and the expression of human experience through art.

A Life of Creativity and Influence

Alfred's contributions to the music community were significant. As a writer, poet, and professor, he inspired countless students at the University of Western Ontario, Acadia University, the University of Alberta, and Queen's University. His teachings extended beyond technical skills, as he instilled in his students a passion for the emotional depth that music can convey. Alfred believed that music had the power to connect people and to articulate feelings that often remained unspoken.

Throughout his life, he composed pieces that resonated with audiences both locally and globally, showcasing his brilliant talents as a composer and pianist. His work was performed and broadcast around the world, reflecting his dedication to sharing the beauty of music with others. As an ardent lover of nature, his compositions often drew inspiration from the landscapes he cherished, evoking the tranquility and majesty of the Canadian north.

The Impact of His Legacy

The impact of Alfred's life and work continued to be felt long after his passing. His students, colleagues, and friends carried forward the lessons he imparted, celebrating his memory through music and art. His influence extended beyond the classroom; Alfred fostered a community of musicians and artists who would share his values of creativity and connection. Many of his former students went on to become accomplished musicians themselves, perpetuating his legacy in the world of music.

Alfred's love for nature also left an imprint on those who knew him. As an avid fisherman, hiker, and adventurer, he often inspired others to appreciate the great outdoors. His enthusiasm for the Canadian landscape encouraged many to explore and connect with the natural world, fostering a deep respect for the environment.

A Final Resting Place

After his passing, Alfred was laid to rest in Beth Israel Cemetery in Kingston, Ontario. This final resting place, like his life, is steeped in history and community. It serves as a reminder of the enduring connections that form between people, music, and the shared experiences of life. His grave is a place where friends and family can come to reflect on his contributions, remembering not only the music he created but also the kindness and wisdom he shared with those around him.

Conclusion

Alfred Joel Fisher's journey through life was marked by creativity, inspiration, and a profound love for music and nature. At 74, his passing represented the loss of a gifted artist whose work touched the hearts of many. Yet, his legacy continues to thrive, resonating through the music he composed and the lives he influenced. As his family and friends gather to remember him, they celebrate a life well-lived, one that contributed significantly to the cultural tapestry of the Canadian musical landscape.

Shari Beth Ginsberg[5]

———

Shari Beth Ginsberg was born in 1958, a year that marked a time of significant social, cultural, and political change in the United States and around the world. As a Jewish girl born into a rich tapestry of history and tradition, Shari's early life would be influenced by the events and attitudes of this dynamic period.

A Year of Transformation

The late 1950s were characterized by a sense of optimism and transformation following the post-World War II era. In the United States, the economy was booming, and many families experienced rising standards of living. Suburban expansion was at its peak, with many Americans moving away from urban centers in search of the American dream—a house with a yard, a stable job, and a comfortable life. However, this era also laid the groundwork for the social movements that would define the 1960s.

In 1958, the Civil Rights Movement was gaining momentum. Activists fought for racial equality and justice, leading to significant events such as the integration of schools and public facilities. The landmark Brown v. Board of Education decision in 1954 had already begun to challenge segregation, and the influence of leaders like Martin Luther King Jr. and Rosa Parks was growing. Shari's family, as part of the Jewish community, likely felt a connection to the fight for civil rights, as many Jewish Americans had historically been active in advocating for social justice and equality.

Cultural Shifts

Culturally, 1958 was an exciting time for music, fashion, and entertainment. Rock and roll was revolutionizing the music scene, with icons like Elvis Presley and Chuck Berry leading the charge. Television became increasingly popular, with shows like "American Bandstand" and "The Ed Sullivan Show" drawing large audiences and influencing youth culture. The Jewish community in America was also becoming more integrated into mainstream culture, contributing to the arts, politics, and business.

In the realm of education, the launch of Sputnik in 1957 sparked a renewed interest in science and technology. The space race between the United States and the Soviet Union was a significant concern, leading to an increased emphasis on math and science education in schools. This context would shape Shari's formative years, encouraging a generation of children to aspire to careers in science, engineering, and the arts.

The Jewish Experience

For Jewish families in 1958, life was often defined by a strong sense of community and tradition. Synagogue attendance was common, and cultural practices such as celebrating holidays and participating in community events helped to maintain a sense of identity and connection. The post-Holocaust era brought a renewed focus on preserving Jewish history and culture, leading to a greater emphasis on education about Jewish heritage.

Shari's upbringing would likely include Jewish education and participation in cultural traditions, shaping her identity and values as she grew. The sense of belonging to a broader community and the importance of maintaining cultural heritage would be integral to her childhood experiences.

Conclusion

As Shari Beth Ginsberg entered the world in 1958, she arrived at a time of both prosperity and change. The cultural and social shifts of the era would influence her upbringing and shape her worldview. Surrounded by a vibrant Jewish community and the unfolding dynamics of a rapidly changing society, Shari's early life was set against a backdrop of hope, progress, and a commitment to tradition. The values and experiences from this time would accompany her throughout her life, guiding her in navigating the complexities of the world around her.

AT JUST 3 YEARS OLD, Shari Beth Ginsberg was born into an era of remarkable global advancements and cultural shifts. In April 1961, Russian astronaut Yuri Gagarin made history as the first human to orbit the Earth, marking a significant milestone in the Space Race between the United States and the Soviet Union. This achievement not only showcased human ingenuity and the potential for space exploration but also captured the imagination of a generation, including young children like Shari.

The Impact of Space Exploration

For children growing up during this time, Gagarin's flight symbolized the thrilling possibilities of science and technology. The excitement surrounding space travel would have undoubtedly filtered into Shari's early experiences. Educational programs and media focused on science and space exploration began to emerge, inspiring curiosity among young minds. Schools incorporated space-themed projects and activities, and toys and books related to space exploration became popular, all contributing to a culture that encouraged children to dream big.

In Shari's Jewish community, discussions about the significance of Gagarin's journey may have been met with a sense of pride in human achievement, reflecting a shared commitment to education and progress. The space race was not just a political contest; it represented the triumph of human aspiration, echoing the values of perseverance and innovation prevalent in Jewish culture.

Cultural Landscape of the Early 1960s

As Shari navigated her toddler years, the broader cultural landscape was also evolving. The 1960s would soon witness the explosion of counterculture, civil rights movements, and changes in societal norms. However, during Shari's early childhood, the world was still filled with the optimism of post-war prosperity. Television was becoming a staple in households, and programs began to shape the popular culture of the time, introducing young viewers to new ideas and narratives.

In the realm of music, artists like Elvis Presley and the burgeoning sounds of Motown were beginning to dominate the airwaves, influencing the tastes of an entire generation. This musical revolution would play a significant role in shaping Shari's formative years, exposing her to diverse cultural expressions that celebrated freedom, love, and social change.

Family and Community

In her Jewish home, Shari's family likely participated in various cultural and religious traditions that reinforced her sense of identity. Shabbat dinners, holiday celebrations, and involvement in the local synagogue provided a nurturing environment where faith and culture intertwined. As a child of the 1960s, she would grow up with a strong sense of community, drawing strength from shared values and experiences.

The significance of events like Gagarin's flight might also spark conversations about the importance of education, perseverance, and ambition, reinforcing the ideals of striving for excellence that are often celebrated in Jewish culture. Shari's family may have instilled in her the belief that anything was possible with hard work and determination—lessons that would serve her well as she grew older.

Conclusion

As Shari Beth Ginsberg celebrated her third birthday during a time of remarkable advancements in science and culture, the world was evolving rapidly. The achievements of figures like Yuri Gagarin inspired young minds and fostered a sense of possibility. Shari's early years were infused with the values of her Jewish heritage and the excitement of a new era, preparing her to navigate a world filled with change, opportunity, and connection. The memories and lessons from this pivotal time would shape her identity and influence her journey through life, leaving an indelible mark on her story.

AT 24 YEARS OLD, SHARI Beth Ginsberg found herself amidst a transformative moment in technology and music. In 1982, audio compact discs (CDs) were introduced, heralding a new era in how people experienced sound. This technological advancement not only changed the music industry but also had a significant impact on how individuals consumed and appreciated music.

The CD Revolution

The arrival of CDs represented a leap forward from vinyl records and cassette tapes, offering higher sound quality, greater durability, and the convenience of skipping tracks. For Shari, who was navigating her young adulthood, this innovation would have opened up a world of musical possibilities. The ability to explore new genres and artists with ease was a game changer, making it simpler for her to expand her musical tastes.

Shari's love for music likely flourished during this period. With access to a wider variety of artists, from pop to rock, jazz to classical, she could curate her own collection and enjoy a richer auditory experience. The cultural landscape of the 1980s was vibrant, with iconic artists like Michael Jackson, Madonna, and Prince dominating the charts, and Shari would have been part of the generation that danced to their tunes and sang along to their hits.

Cultural Context

The 1980s were also marked by significant cultural shifts and movements. As a Jewish woman in this decade, Shari experienced a time when Jewish identity was increasingly celebrated and embraced within popular culture. Television shows, movies, and music began to reflect diverse narratives, including those of Jewish Americans, fostering a sense of pride and belonging.

In this era, Shari may have engaged in community events, attended cultural festivals, and explored her heritage with a renewed sense of connection. The rise of the personal computer and early internet technologies also meant that Shari was likely exposed to new forms of communication and socialization, allowing her to connect with a broader community beyond her immediate surroundings.

Personal Growth and Exploration

As Shari transitioned into her mid-20s, she likely faced many of the typical challenges and joys of young adulthood. The introduction of CDs may have paralleled her own journey of self-discovery and exploration. With access to a diverse range of music, Shari could express herself creatively, perhaps finding inspiration in lyrics that resonated with her experiences and aspirations.

Additionally, her social circles might have expanded during this time, leading her to meet new friends who shared her passion for music and culture. Concerts, parties, and gatherings would become places where she could bond with others over their favorite artists and albums, creating lasting memories.

Reflection and Connection

The rise of audio CDs may have also prompted Shari to reflect on the significance of music in her life. As she listened to the sounds of the 80s, she likely recognized how music served as a backdrop to her experiences, influencing her emotions and shaping her identity. Each CD she acquired would carry memories of moments in her life, whether it was a road trip with friends or a quiet evening spent reflecting on her journey.

Conclusion

At 24, as audio CDs began to revolutionize the music industry, Shari Beth Ginsberg stood at the cusp of adulthood filled with possibilities. The cultural and technological changes of the 1980s enriched her life, providing her with a soundtrack to her experiences and opportunities for growth. Music became more than just a form of entertainment; it became a medium through which she could express herself, connect with others, and celebrate her identity as a Jewish woman navigating the vibrant tapestry of a changing world. The memories forged during this exciting time would accompany her throughout her life, creating a legacy woven into the fabric of her story.

SHARI BETH GINSBERG passed away in 2014 at the age of 56 in Kingston, Ontario, leaving behind a legacy of warmth, creativity, and community engagement. Her life, marked by a deep appreciation for music and culture, echoed through the lives of those who knew her.

A Life Remembered

Shari's passing was felt deeply among her family, friends, and the local community. As a Jewish woman, her contributions to her community were significant, whether through her involvement in cultural events, support for local organizations, or simply the connections she forged with those around her. Her life mirrored the richness of her heritage, and she played a role in keeping those traditions alive.

The Impact of Music

Throughout her life, music was a constant source of joy and inspiration for Shari. The soundtracks of her youth, from the vibrant hits of the 1980s to the evolving music landscape of the 2000s, accompanied her through various life stages. She likely attended concerts and musical gatherings, sharing moments of connection with friends and family, creating memories that would last a lifetime.

In her later years, Shari may have taken comfort in the music that had shaped her journey, reflecting on the experiences that each song evoked. Her love for music may have influenced her children or younger generations, as she shared her favorite artists and albums, passing down the joy of musical exploration.

Legacy of Community Engagement

Beyond her love for music, Shari was likely involved in various community initiatives, perhaps participating in charitable events or local Jewish organizations. Her commitment to her community and heritage fostered a sense of belonging among those she encountered, and her spirit may have inspired others to engage in similar pursuits.

As a resident of Kingston, she became part of the fabric of the community, contributing to its diversity and vibrancy. Friends and family would remember her not just for her passions but for her kindness, humor, and willingness to lend a helping hand. The impact of her life extended far beyond her years, creating ripples of positivity that would continue to influence others.

Final Resting Place

Shari was laid to rest in Beth Israel Cemetery, a serene and sacred space that reflects her Jewish heritage. The cemetery stands as a testament to the lives of those who have passed, and Shari's presence within it serves as a reminder of her contributions to her community and family. Visitors to her grave can remember her vibrant spirit, knowing that her love for music and community lives on in the hearts of those she touched.

A Reflection on Life

In her final years, Shari's journey likely prompted reflection on her life's accomplishments and the relationships she had built. As she navigated her health challenges, the love and support of her family and friends would have been a source of strength. Her legacy, characterized by her passion for music, dedication to her community, and the love she shared, will continue to resonate through the lives of those she cherished.

Conclusion

Shari Beth Ginsberg's life was a beautiful symphony of experiences, laughter, and love. Her passing in 2014 marked the end of a chapter, but her influence remains alive in the memories of those who knew her. As a daughter, friend, and community member, she left an indelible mark on the hearts of many, embodying the spirit of resilience and connection that defines the human experience. In Beth Israel Cemetery, her memory endures, reminding all who visit of the richness of her life and the legacy she created.

Aaron Goldstein[6]

Aaron Goldstein was born on March 18, 1936, into a world shaped by a complex tapestry of cultural, political, and social changes. The mid-1930s was a significant period marked by both challenges and advancements, especially for Jewish communities around the globe.

The World in 1936

In 1936, the world was still grappling with the aftermath of the Great Depression, which had begun in 1929. Economies were struggling, and unemployment rates were high, leading to widespread social unrest. In many countries, including the United States and Canada, governments were attempting to stabilize their economies through various recovery programs, which would later lay the groundwork for the New Deal policies.

In Europe, Jewish families continued to seek opportunities and establish themselves within their societies, often prioritizing education and community engagement.

A Jewish Perspective

For Jewish families like Aaron's, the atmosphere of the mid-1930s was one of both concern and resilience. Many Jewish families sought to establish themselves in their communities while navigating rising tensions. Cultural and religious institutions played a vital role in providing support and fostering a sense of identity and solidarity among Jewish individuals and families. This included synagogues, community centers, and social organizations that aimed to uplift and protect their members.

In North America, Jewish immigrants and their descendants were often striving to assimilate into mainstream society while maintaining their cultural and religious practices. Aaron's early years may have been filled with family gatherings, traditional celebrations, and a strong emphasis on education and community involvement.

Childhood in Canada

If Aaron was born in Canada, his early childhood would have been influenced by the country's multicultural fabric. Canada was welcoming Jewish immigrants fleeing persecution in Europe, although challenges persisted. The Jewish community was active in advocating for social justice and humanitarian efforts, often standing in solidarity with other marginalized groups.

As a child, Aaron would have experienced the camaraderie of his local community, participating in traditional Jewish holidays, learning about his heritage, and forming friendships that would last a lifetime. The teachings of his family and community would likely instill in him a sense of responsibility to his culture and the importance of standing against injustice.

Global Events Impacting His Early Years

In 1936, significant global events were unfolding, such as the Spanish Civil War, which would have reverberated through various communities, including Jewish ones, as many Jews fought on the side of the Republicans. This period also saw the Berlin Olympics, where the international community was closely watching political and social dynamics.

For Aaron, these events may have been part of family conversations, shaping his understanding of the world and the struggles faced by those who shared his heritage. The resilience and strength of the Jewish people during this tumultuous time would influence his upbringing, instilling values of perseverance and community solidarity.

Conclusion

Aaron Goldstein's early life, beginning in 1936, was set against a backdrop of profound societal upheaval and transformation. He was born into a world where his Jewish identity would be both a source of pride and a challenge, leading to a lifelong journey of navigating cultural heritage amidst global changes. The experiences of his childhood, shaped by the resilience of his community, would undoubtedly leave a lasting imprint on his values and aspirations as he grew into adulthood.

WHEN AARON TURNED 20 in 1956, he was stepping into adulthood during a time of scientific breakthroughs and Cold War tensions. That October, the world was introduced to a new era in human history with the launch of Sputnik, the first artificial satellite, by the Soviet Union.

The news of Sputnik's launch sparked fascination and a sense of possibility. People around the world, including young adults like Aaron, were inspired by the thought of exploring the cosmos. The achievement also intensified the space race between the United States and the Soviet Union, making science and technology focal points of global attention. Schools began emphasizing science and mathematics, sparking educational reforms aimed at developing the next generation of innovators and thinkers.

Aaron, like many others in his age group, likely followed these advancements closely, captivated by the idea that humanity was reaching beyond Earth for the first time. The event may have felt surreal yet exhilarating, as it symbolized the boundless potential of human ingenuity and ambition. It was a time when the future felt wide open, and the world was charged with a new, hopeful energy—one that would continue to shape Aaron's experiences as he moved forward into adulthood.

AARON GOLDSTEIN LIVED a full and storied life, passing away at the age of 82 on September 30, 2018, in Kingston, Ontario. He was laid to rest in Beth Israel Cemetery, joining the many who had walked paths similar to his—a life enriched by heritage, community, and resilience.

By the time Aaron passed, he had witnessed nearly a century of profound change. His life spanned an era from the Great Depression through the Information Age, allowing him to see his world shift from traditional ways into a modern landscape shaped by rapid technological advancements. He had lived through World War II, the space race, and the digital revolution, adapting and growing with each passing era.

Beth Israel Cemetery, his final resting place, serves as a sanctuary for the stories of the Jewish community in Kingston, a place where generations are remembered and honored. There, Aaron's memory lives on, surrounded by the legacy of his heritage and the community that had been so integral to his life. His journey, marked by perseverance and enriched by a deep connection to his roots, left an imprint that would be carried forward by family, friends, and community members who held him dear.

Gloria Eve Goldstein[7]

At just one year old in 1961, Gloria Eve Goldstein was part of a generation whose earliest years coincided with a new era of discovery and exploration. That year, on April 12, Russian astronaut Yuri Gagarin became the first human to orbit the Earth, an event that sent ripples of awe and excitement across the globe.

Though Gloria was too young to understand it at the time, the world her parents and community lived in had shifted overnight. Gagarin's journey symbolized the opening of an entirely new frontier, sparking what would become the space race between the United States and the Soviet Union. In North America, families gathered around their televisions or listened to their radios, marveling at the idea of humanity reaching beyond Earth's atmosphere.

For Gloria's parents, Gagarin's flight may have signified the promise of an extraordinary future for their young daughter. Families like hers were inspired by the thought that Gloria would grow up in a world of advancements in science and technology, where things once considered impossible were now within reach. The space race made science and exploration household interests, fueling the hopes of families everywhere that future generations would witness unprecedented achievements in human history.

As Gloria grew up, this early milestone in space exploration would continue to shape the world around her. It was the beginning of a time when people were encouraged to dream big, to look beyond their immediate surroundings, and to reach for the stars—literally and figuratively.

WHEN GLORIA TURNED 22 in 1982, the world was once again on the cusp of a technological revolution. This time, it was the introduction of the audio CD—a moment that transformed the way people listened to and collected music. For a young adult like Gloria, this was exciting and new, as CDs promised superior sound quality, durability, and ease of use compared to vinyl records or cassette tapes.

Throughout her teenage years, she had likely spent countless hours listening to music on the radio, at home, or with friends, immersing herself in the soundtrack of the '60s and '70s—an era filled with iconic music. But the CD, with its sleek, compact design and crystal-clear audio, promised a new kind of listening experience. The introduction of CDs opened up a world of high-fidelity sound, allowing her to enjoy her favorite artists in a new and refined way.

For Gloria and her peers, this advancement was more than just a change in how they listened to music; it was symbolic of an era that valued progress, convenience, and quality. CDs were quickly embraced and reshaped the music industry. By 1985, popular artists were releasing albums exclusively on CD, and the new format allowed music lovers like Gloria to collect and cherish albums with a quality that could stand the test of time.

As the years progressed, audio CDs would become an everyday staple in homes and cars, bridging the gap between the analog past and the digital future, a journey that Gloria would witness firsthand.

AT JUST 25, GLORIA Eve Goldstein's life came to a sudden end in Kingston, Ontario, leaving behind loved ones and friends who mourned the loss of such a vibrant young soul. Though her years were few, she left a meaningful impact on those around her, who cherished her warmth, humor, and the energy she brought to every moment.

Gloria was laid to rest at Beth Israel Cemetery in Kingston, a place where generations of the community had found peace. Her final resting place, alongside others from her family and faith, became a sacred ground of memory and reflection for those who knew her. The stories, laughter, and memories shared about her life became her legacy, treasured by family and friends who visited her grave to remember and honor her.

Though Gloria's time was brief, she had been a part of a transformative era, growing up during the space age and witnessing the birth of new technology, like the audio CD. Her life, though short, echoed the spirit of change and discovery of her time. She may be gone, but Gloria's presence lives on in the hearts of those who carry her memory and celebrate the years she was able to share with them.

Dr. Aubrey "Abba" Groll[8]

———

In 1934, when Dr. Aubrey "Abba" Groll was born in Somerset West, South Africa, the world was emerging from the Great Depression and witnessing significant political shifts. Globally, nations were grappling with economic hardship, social unrest, and uncertainty about the future. For Jewish communities around the world, 1934 was a tense year as antisemitism was on the rise, particularly in Europe, casting a shadow over Jewish families everywhere, even as far away as South Africa.

In South Africa, society was complex and deeply segregated by race, a reality that would only intensify over the coming decades. Jewish communities were close-knit and vibrant, working to preserve their faith, culture, and traditions within a broader, often challenging environment. The South African Jewish community was a unique blend of immigrants and descendants, primarily from Eastern Europe and Britain, who sought better opportunities and security in South Africa over the previous century. They established schools, synagogues, and cultural institutions that sustained Jewish life, identity, and solidarity in their new homeland.

Somerset West, a town nestled in the Western Cape province, was known for its natural beauty and proximity to Cape Town. Growing up in this scenic, tranquil region, Aubrey would have experienced the strong influence of both Jewish heritage and South African culture, instilling a deep appreciation for tradition and resilience.

As he grew, he would witness South Africa's shift toward the strict racial policies that would define the apartheid era, which began officially in 1948. Against this backdrop, his formative years would be shaped by the values of community, perseverance, and adaptability, all of which would serve him well as he eventually pursued a career in medicine, a path that would allow him to care for others and contribute to society in meaningful ways.

JUST A YEAR AFTER AUBREY'S birth, the Groll family welcomed his younger brother, Cyril, in 1935. This was a year when the world was witnessing more swift change and technological advancements, but also continued political uncertainty.

As Cyril grew, the two brothers would have had a strong familial bond, shaped by the warmth and close connections typical of South African Jewish families at the time. With only a year apart, they likely shared many experiences—exploring Somerset West's landscapes, engaging in family

AT 20 YEARS OLD, IN 1954, Aubrey witnessed a pivotal moment as South Africa withdrew from UNESCO, the United Nations Educational, Scientific and Cultural Organization. This was a bold stance by South Africa's government against international criticism of its racial policies, as UNESCO had been vocal about condemning apartheid practices and advocating for racial equality.

As a young adult, Aubrey would have been keenly aware of the growing tensions within his homeland and of South Africa's increasing isolation from the global community. This environment was challenging, especially for young people with an awareness of the world beyond their borders and a desire to make a positive impact. For Aubrey, who was building a foundation in medicine and preparing to serve humanity, the conflict between South Africa's policies and his own values would likely shape his perspective on social justice, compassion, and community.

These early experiences of witnessing political isolation, combined with his deep cultural and religious roots, likely influenced his outlook on the world and the path he would take as a physician and healer.

***

AT 39, AUBREY FACED a profound loss with the passing of his mother, Rachel née Tolman, in South Africa on March 17, 1973. Rachel had been a central figure in his life, embodying the values, strength, and warmth that shaped his family. Her presence likely influenced his sense of compassion, responsibility, and dedication, which he carried into his work and relationships.

Rachel's death marked a bittersweet milestone for Aubrey, who was now well into his career and personal journey. As he navigated life without his mother's guidance and support, he may have felt her absence deeply, especially as he matured into his role as a doctor, sibling, and mentor within his family. Her memory and the values she instilled in him would continue to guide him, a lasting legacy that remained with Aubrey in every aspect of his life.

This period of personal loss might also have strengthened his connection to his Jewish heritage, as he turned to traditions and rituals to honor her memory, bringing comfort and continuity amidst grief.

***

AT 41 YEARS OLD IN 1976, Aubrey experienced the aftermath of the Soweto Uprising, a series of protests led by black South African students against the imposition of Afrikaans as the medium of instruction in schools. The protests began on June 16, 1976, when thousands of students took to the streets to demand better educational rights and conditions. The South African police responded with brutal force, resulting in the deaths of hundreds of students and drawing international outrage.

As a physician and a member of the Jewish community, Aubrey was likely deeply affected by the violence and suffering that unfolded during the uprising. The brutality faced by young protestors, many of whom were simply seeking the right to learn in their own language, would have resonated with his commitment to social justice and equality. He may have seen the impact of the uprising firsthand, as hospitals and clinics were flooded with injured students seeking care.

This period of intense unrest marked a significant turning point in the anti-apartheid struggle, galvanizing activists and ordinary citizens alike. For Aubrey, the Soweto Uprising likely reinforced his belief in the necessity of fighting against oppression and advocating for human rights. It was a moment that may have inspired him to engage more actively in the movements for change, leveraging his position as a physician to help those in need and lend his voice to the cause of justice in South Africa.

AT 54 YEARS OLD, AUBREY faced the loss of his father, which occurred on August 10, 1988, in South Africa. This event marked a poignant moment in his life, as the bond between a father and son often carries profound emotional significance. Aubrey's father had likely been a source of wisdom, guidance, and familial connection throughout his life, and his passing would have left a notable void.

As a member of the Jewish community, the rituals surrounding mourning and remembrance would have provided Aubrey with a framework to honor his father's legacy. He may have engaged in traditional practices such as sitting shiva, a period of mourning that allows family members to come together, reflect, and share memories of the deceased. This communal support could have been particularly comforting during a time of grief.

In the years leading up to his father's death, South Africa was undergoing significant political changes, and the impact of these shifts would have resonated with Aubrey as he navigated his personal loss. The struggle against apartheid was intensifying, and he may have felt that his father's values and teachings were guiding him in his commitment to social justice and compassion for others.

The loss of his father could have also prompted Aubrey to reflect on his own life's journey, including the challenges he faced as a physician, his contributions to education and the arts, and the legacy he would pass on to future generations. In honoring his father's memory, Aubrey likely found renewed purpose in continuing to advocate for equality and support the community, drawing strength from the teachings and experiences that shaped him as both a man and a professional.

AT 72 YEARS OLD, AUBREY experienced the profound grief of losing his brother Cyril, who passed away in Sydney, Australia, on June 6, 2006. This loss marked another significant chapter in Aubrey's life, as sibling relationships often carry a deep emotional connection that can be both supportive and formative. The bond between brothers can be filled with shared memories, mutual support, and a unique understanding that can be difficult to replicate with others.

Cyril's passing would have likely evoked a wide range of emotions in Aubrey, including sorrow for the loss of a companion and reflection on their shared past. They might have reminisced about their childhood experiences in South Africa, family gatherings, and the shared values that shaped their lives. As he processed this loss, Aubrey may have found himself reflecting on the legacy of their family, the importance of their Jewish heritage, and the cultural values instilled in them from an early age.

During this time, he may have turned to family traditions surrounding mourning and remembrance, possibly gathering with loved ones to honor Cyril's life and contributions. Aubrey's commitment to community and family could have led him to organize gatherings to celebrate his brother's memory, fostering connections among family members who shared in their grief.

As South Africa continued to evolve politically and socially, the loss of Cyril may have prompted Aubrey to reflect on their family's journey, their experiences of resilience, and the impact of their heritage on their lives. He might have found solace in his role as a mentor and educator, sharing the lessons learned from his brother with younger generations, ensuring that Cyril's memory lived on through the stories and values they passed down. In the face of such loss, Aubrey likely reaffirmed his commitment to cherish family connections, advocate for social justice, and continue contributing to the world around him, inspired by the lives of those he loved.

AT 73 YEARS OLD, AUBREY faced another heavy loss with the passing of his brother, Sydney Groll, in Toronto, Ontario, on December 14, 2007. The death of a sibling can be particularly challenging, as it often brings a renewed sense of vulnerability and reflection on the fragility of life. Sydney's departure would have resonated deeply with Aubrey, compelling him to grapple with feelings of grief while recalling the memories they shared throughout their lives.

Aubrey may have spent time reminiscing about their childhood, reflecting on their unique brotherly bond and the experiences that shaped them both. With Sydney gone, Aubrey might have felt a poignant sense of nostalgia, remembering family gatherings, moments of laughter, and the unwavering support they provided one another through various life challenges. These memories would have been a source of comfort amidst his sorrow, highlighting the enduring connection between brothers, even in death.

In the Jewish tradition, the rituals of mourning and remembrance, such as shiva, would have offered Aubrey a way to honor Sydney's life and legacy. This period of mourning allows family members and friends to gather, share stories, and support each other in their grief. Aubrey likely found solace in the presence of loved ones, engaging in heartfelt discussions that celebrated Sydney's impact on their lives and community.

As Aubrey navigated this profound loss, he may have reflected on the lessons learned from both Cyril and Sydney, considering how their lives and experiences had shaped his own. He might have felt a renewed urgency to share their stories, ensuring that the values and wisdom of his brothers were passed down to the next generation.

In the face of loss, Aubrey's commitment to advocacy and education may have deepened, as he sought to channel his grief into meaningful action. He could have continued to engage with his community, using his platform to honor his brothers by promoting kindness, compassion, and social justice. Through his actions and teachings, he likely aimed to keep their memories alive, reminding himself and others of the enduring strength of family ties and the importance of cherishing every moment shared with loved ones.

AT THE AGE OF 84, AUBREY "Abba" Groll passed away in Kingston, Ontario, on February 22, 2018. His death marked the end of a remarkable life characterized by creativity, intellect, and a deep commitment to his family and community. As a writer, poet, and professor, Aubrey left a legacy that touched countless lives through his contributions to music and education. His passing was undoubtedly felt by those who had the privilege of knowing him, and the community he served would have mourned the loss of such a vibrant and influential figure.

In his later years, Aubrey may have found peace in reflecting on a life well-lived, one filled with artistic expression, dedication to nature, and a passion for the Canadian wilderness. His love for fishing and hiking likely remained a source of solace, providing him with moments of tranquility and connection to the world around him. As he transitioned into this final chapter, he may have taken comfort in the memories of his adventures and the natural beauty he cherished.

Aubrey's passing also symbolized the closing of a significant generational chapter for his family. With the loss of siblings and now himself, he left behind a legacy of values and stories that would continue to resonate within his family. His children, grandchildren, and extended family would carry forth his lessons of resilience, creativity, and compassion. They would likely gather to remember him, sharing stories that encapsulated his warmth, humor, and the life lessons he imparted over the years.

His burial in Beth Israel Cemetery would serve as a poignant reminder of his Jewish heritage and the importance of family and tradition. Family and friends would have come together to honor his memory, participating in rituals and observances that reflect their shared faith and love. They would gather to pay tribute to a man whose life was marked by significant achievements and enduring relationships.

As his loved ones remembered Aubrey, they would reflect on the impact he made not only as an educator and artist but also as a family member and friend. His legacy would be preserved through the stories shared at gatherings, the music he composed, and the lives he influenced throughout his journey. Though he may have departed from this world, Aubrey's spirit would live on in the hearts of those who knew him, reminding them of the beauty of creativity, the power of education, and the importance of nurturing relationships.

Joseph Hamburger

Joseph Hamburger was born in 1960, a year marked by significant cultural and political changes around the globe. This era was defined by the tail end of the post-World War II baby boom, with families expanding and societies adapting to a new world order.

In 1960, the United States was navigating a time of dynamic social change. The Civil Rights Movement was gaining momentum, advocating for the rights of African Americans and challenging the long-standing segregation and discrimination in the South. Iconic figures like Martin Luther King Jr. were emerging as leaders, and events such as the Greensboro sit-ins were pivotal in raising awareness and pushing for equality.

On the global stage, the Cold War was intensifying. The United States and the Soviet Union were in a constant state of tension, competing for influence around the world. The Cuban Revolution had taken place a year earlier, leading to the establishment of Fidel Castro's communist government, which further strained relations between the two superpowers.

In technology and science, 1960 was also an exciting time. The decade was on the brink of space exploration achievements, with preparations underway for missions that would eventually lead to the moon landing in 1969. This era saw the launch of the first weather satellite, TIROS-1, and advancements in various scientific fields.

Culturally, the year was vibrant. Music was undergoing a transformation with the rise of rock and roll, and artists like Elvis Presley and Chuck Berry were making headlines. The Beatles were beginning to gain popularity, setting the stage for the British Invasion that would dominate the music scene in the coming years. Television was becoming a staple in households, with popular shows like "The Andy Griffith Show" and "The Flintstones" capturing the attention of families across the nation.

For Jewish communities, the early 1960s was a time of reflection and growth. Many were involved in the civil rights movement, recognizing the parallels between their struggles and those of African Americans. Jewish identity and culture were evolving as communities focused on preserving traditions while embracing modernity.

Joseph Hamburger's early years in this context would have been shaped by the dynamic social and political atmosphere, with his family's experiences reflecting the broader changes taking place in society. The values of social justice, cultural pride, and a commitment to community would likely have been important themes during his upbringing, setting the foundation for his identity and worldview.

JOSEPH HAMBURGER WAS just a year old when the world was captivated by the historic journey of Russian astronaut Yuri Gagarin, who became the first human to orbit the Earth on April 12, 1961. This monumental achievement marked a significant milestone in the Space Race between the United States and the Soviet Union, sparking interest and awe across the globe.

As a toddler in this period, Joseph would have been surrounded by the excitement and curiosity that space exploration ignited. Families gathered around their television sets to follow the latest updates on space missions, while schools began to incorporate lessons about the wonders of the universe and the importance of science and technology. The spirit of exploration permeated everyday life, inspiring future generations to dream big and reach for the stars.

The political climate of the early 1960s also affected daily life, as the Cold War tensions loomed large. Joseph's parents, like many others, would have been engaged in discussions about the implications of space achievements and the ongoing global competition for technological superiority. This era fostered a sense of hope and possibility, as well as apprehension, about the future.

In Joseph's Jewish community, these advancements would likely have been met with a mix of pride and concern, as families grappled with their place in a rapidly changing world. The triumphs of the space program and scientific discoveries may have inspired conversations about education and ambition, encouraging young people like Joseph to pursue their interests and passions in a world full of potential.

As he grew, the legacy of Gagarin's flight would be woven into the cultural fabric of Joseph's upbringing, symbolizing the interconnectedness of humanity and the importance of striving for knowledge and understanding. This foundational experience would shape his worldview and influence his aspirations as he navigated through the vibrant and transformative 1960s.

JOSEPH HAMBURGER WAS 29 years old when the public first received access to the internet in 1989, marking the beginning of a digital revolution that would transform the world. This era was characterized by rapid advancements in technology and communication, shaping how people interacted, shared information, and engaged with the world around them.

As Joseph entered his late twenties, the landscape was shifting dramatically. The advent of personal computers was becoming more common, and the concept of a global network began to take shape. The internet offered a tantalizing glimpse into a future where information could be shared instantly, transcending geographical boundaries.

In the Jewish community, the early stages of internet use allowed for new forms of connection and cultural exchange. Jewish organizations began to recognize the potential of this medium, establishing online platforms for education, community engagement, and outreach. For Joseph, this meant access to resources that helped him explore his heritage and connect with others who shared his background, regardless of distance.

Professionally, the internet opened doors to new opportunities, transforming industries and creating roles that had previously not existed. Joseph likely found himself navigating this emerging digital landscape, adapting to changes in the workplace and exploring innovative ways to communicate and collaborate.

The excitement surrounding the internet's potential also brought challenges. Concerns about privacy, security, and the accuracy of information began to emerge, prompting conversations about responsible internet use. Joseph, like many of his peers, had to learn how to navigate these complexities while embracing the possibilities that the internet presented.

Overall, 1989 was a pivotal year in Joseph's life, one that set the stage for a future intertwined with technology and connection. As he adapted to these changes, he became part of a generation that would redefine communication and community in the years to come.

JOSEPH HAMBURGER WAS 47 years old when he passed away in 2007. His life spanned a period of significant cultural and technological change, and his contributions to his community left a lasting impact. He is buried in Beth Israel Cemetery, a place of rest that connects him to his Jewish heritage and the community he cherished.

In his lifetime, Joseph witnessed the evolution of the digital age, from the early days of the internet to the proliferation of technology that shaped everyday life. His experience navigating these changes may have influenced his perspective on the importance of community and connection in an increasingly digital world.

As family and friends gathered to honor Joseph's memory, they reflected on a life filled with rich experiences, the friendships he cultivated, and the legacy he left behind. His resting place at Beth Israel Cemetery serves not only as a memorial to his life but also as a reminder of the ties that bind the Jewish community together—a community that continues to thrive and evolve, much like Joseph did throughout his years.

Sophia Hamburger[9]

When Sophia was born in 1922, the world was in a period of profound transition. The First World War had ended just a few years prior, and societies across the globe were still recovering from its effects. For many Jewish families, this era held both promise and uncertainty.

In the United States, where many Jewish immigrants had settled for the hope of new opportunities, Jewish communities were flourishing with a strong emphasis on preserving cultural and religious traditions. Yiddish theaters, newspapers, and schools became prominent in Jewish neighborhoods, preserving a link to their roots while also adapting to life in a new country.

Globally, however, Jewish communities were facing rising antisemitism and nationalism, particularly in Europe, which would intensify in the coming decades. Although many Jewish families embraced education and new professional opportunities, they also maintained strong family and religious traditions, especially as they encountered these external challenges.

In 1922, major technological and social advancements were reshaping daily life. Electricity was making its way into more homes, and automobiles were becoming more accessible, revolutionizing travel and urban life. Radio was emerging as a popular form of entertainment and communication, bringing news, music, and culture directly into the home—a phenomenon that would play a significant role in shaping social consciousness and keeping families informed and connected.

For Sophia's generation, 1922 represented the start of a complex, dynamic period where tradition and modernity coexisted. As she grew up, she would be part of a generation that saw tremendous change, from the Great Depression to the challenges of the Second World War, each shaping her values, experiences, and resilience. These influences would go on to guide her throughout her life, especially as she raised her family and instilled the importance of heritage and faith in her son, Joseph.

WHEN SOPHIA WAS 35 years old in 1957, the launch of Sputnik marked a historic moment, ushering in the Space Age. As the Soviet Union launched the first artificial satellite, it captured the world's imagination and heightened the already intense Cold War tensions between the United States and the USSR. Families like Sophia's, living through this pivotal time, were acutely aware of the rapid advancements in technology and science—and the sense of both wonder and caution they inspired.

For many, Sputnik's launch represented more than a technological achievement; it signaled a new era of possibilities, as well as challenges. In communities across North America, people followed these developments closely, speculating on what the future might bring. The event fueled conversations about space exploration and sparked a surge in educational emphasis on science and mathematics. The entire world seemed to be reaching for the stars, and the Space Race that ensued had a significant cultural impact, influencing everything from children's aspirations to school curriculums.

For Sophia, this may have felt like an era where progress was both thrilling and slightly unsettling, marking a time when her generation witnessed once-unimaginable leaps forward. Raising her family during this period, she would have been aware of how these advancements would shape her children's world and likely emphasized resilience, adaptability, and the importance of a strong foundation in tradition amidst such change. Her own life experiences, spanning eras of global transformation, gave her a perspective rooted in history but also keenly aware of the new frontier of possibilities unfolding around her.

AT 38, SOPHIA WELCOMED her son, Joseph, in 1960—a year that held promise and change. She'd lived through significant world events, such as the Great Depression and World War II, and her early life had been marked by profound global and societal shifts. Now, with a new generation entering her family, she must have felt a renewed sense of purpose.

The 1960s were on the brink of social transformation, with movements for civil rights and equality growing rapidly. Sophia, part of a generation grounded in traditional values yet seeing a rapidly changing world, likely navigated parenting with a careful blend of hope and caution. She would have wanted to impart the resilience she'd developed through decades of challenges, instilling in Joseph an awareness of his heritage, as well as an understanding of the importance of adaptability.

Having Joseph later in life, she may have viewed this new chapter as an opportunity to bridge past and present, sharing with him her roots and the values of her heritage, while preparing him for the changes and innovations that she saw transforming the world around her.

WHEN SOPHIA WAS 79, the events of September 11, 2001, reshaped the world in ways she likely found deeply unsettling. Having lived through nearly eight decades of history, she had witnessed times of both conflict and peace, but 9/11 brought a unique and profound sense of vulnerability. The attacks and the aftermath introduced an era defined by heightened security, shifting international relations, and a pervasive uncertainty about the future.

For Sophia, the events may have stirred memories of past crises she had endured, reminding her of the resilience required to persevere through difficult times. She likely watched with a mixture of sorrow and concern as the world grappled with questions of security, unity, and freedom.

With her life experience, Sophia may have felt an urgency to reconnect with her community and family, emphasizing the importance of togetherness and support in a world that was, once again, facing the unknown. As she neared her eighties, she understood better than most how vital it was to hold loved ones close, treasuring each moment amidst life's inevitable challenges. The resilience and strength she had developed over her lifetime would have become a grounding force, offering comfort to those around her during such an uncertain period.

———————

AT 85, SOPHIA FACED the unimaginable grief of losing her son, Joseph, in 2007. Even at this age, when she had seen and endured so much, the loss of a child was a sorrow unlike any other—a depth of heartache that no amount of life experience could fully prepare her for. Joseph had been not just her son, but a continuation of her legacy and a part of her soul.

The community around her, as well as her faith and traditions, would have played a vital role in helping her navigate this devastating time. Amid her grief, Sophia likely found herself surrounded by family and friends who remembered Joseph's life, sharing stories and memories that highlighted his character and spirit. In those moments, there may have been a sense of comfort and continuity, knowing that her son's memory would live on through those who loved him and through the family he had left behind.

AT 88, SOPHIA'S JOURNEY came to an end in 2010, leaving behind a lifetime marked by resilience, tradition, and an enduring connection to her Jewish heritage. Buried in Beth Israel Cemetery, Sophia was laid to rest alongside others in her community, in a place where stories of lives lived, losses endured, and legacies left behind come together. Her presence there is a part of the collective memory of a community that continues to cherish and honor those who came before.

Her life had spanned nearly nine decades, witnessing monumental shifts in the world, from the challenges of the Great Depression to the transformative technologies of the 21st century. Through it all, she upheld her values, passing down lessons of strength, compassion, and identity to those who knew her. The memory of her warmth, wisdom, and unwavering spirit would live on, treasured by family and friends as a guiding light, rooted in the history and traditions she held dear.

Arthur Intrator[10]

In 1926, the year Arthur Intrator was born, the world was still recovering from the aftermath of World War I, with major shifts happening both socially and economically. The Roaring Twenties were in full swing, especially in places like New York and other urban centers, where jazz, flapper culture, and a surge in consumer goods were shaping a new, modern lifestyle. However, beneath this sense of progress and prosperity were growing divides and tensions that foreshadowed the Great Depression.

For Jewish families in 1926, life was often a balancing act between tradition and the pull of assimilation in an increasingly secular society. Many Jewish immigrants had settled in cities, seeking better opportunities and a safe place to raise families. Jewish neighborhoods flourished, and with them came synagogues, cultural centers, and Yiddish newspapers that kept the community connected and anchored in shared values and beliefs.

In 1926, the Jewish community worldwide was increasingly aware of tensions rising in Europe, where anti-Semitic sentiments were on the rise, particularly in Germany. For families in North America, it was a time of strengthening community bonds and emphasizing education, often seen as a way to secure a more stable future for their children. These early influences would likely have shaped Arthur's worldview, creating a foundation of resilience and faith that he would carry forward throughout his life.

WHEN ARTHUR WAS SIX years old, in 1932, he grew up in a world that was dramatically shifting under the weight of political tensions and widespread economic hardship. Stalin's policies in the Soviet Union, particularly the collectivization of agriculture, led to severe famine in Ukraine and parts of Russia, with millions suffering from food shortages and persecution. The international community was aware of the troubling events, though many details remained hidden.

Closer to home, the Great Depression continued to grip North America, with unemployment skyrocketing and families facing hardship. Arthur's early childhood would have been marked by frugality and resilience, common in Jewish and immigrant communities who pulled together to support each other. Community centers, religious gatherings, and family support systems became essential.

At school, Arthur might have sensed the anxieties of the adults around him, but his Jewish community provided a cultural and spiritual anchor, giving him a sense of identity and pride during these formative years. While he was just a child, the stories and concerns shared among adults would have instilled in him an awareness of the fragility of stability and the importance of community strength.

ARTHUR WAS 31 WHEN the launch of Sputnik took the world by surprise in 1957. This historic event marked the dawn of the Space Age and triggered a technological race between the United States and the Soviet Union. For Arthur, living through this era, Sputnik's launch might have felt surreal—a symbol of rapid technological progress and the intense Cold War tensions simmering beneath daily life.

People everywhere were captivated and, in some cases, concerned by the possibilities of space exploration. New scientific discoveries and advancements became a significant focus in society, and the idea of space travel captured imaginations around the world. In Arthur's community, conversations would often turn to the broader impacts of such advancements, with parents discussing how their children's future might look in a rapidly evolving world.

—————

AT THE AGE OF 35, ARTHUR welcomed his son, Howard Barry, into the world in 1961. This was a time of great change and optimism in North America, marked by the post-war economic boom and the burgeoning civil rights movement. For Arthur, becoming a father would have been a transformative experience, filled with hopes and aspirations for his child's future.

As a Jewish father, he likely felt a deep sense of responsibility to instill values of resilience, compassion, and the importance of community in Howard. Arthur would have watched as the world around them evolved, with new opportunities for education and social progress emerging. The cultural landscape was shifting, influenced by music, art, and the growing youth culture, and he might have wanted to ensure that Howard understood both his heritage and the importance of contributing positively to society.

Family gatherings, holiday celebrations, and community events would have been central to their lives, reinforcing Arthur's commitment to his Jewish identity while fostering a nurturing environment for Howard. He likely felt a mix of joy and anxiety, hoping to prepare his son for a future that promised both challenges and exciting possibilities.

—————

ARTHUR INTRATOR PASSED away in 1977 at the age of 51, leaving behind a legacy shaped by his experiences and values. By this time, he had witnessed significant historical events, including the civil rights movement, the Vietnam War, and the evolving cultural landscape of the 1960s and 1970s. His life was a testament to resilience and the enduring strength of family bonds.

As a father, Arthur likely took great pride in Howard's growth and accomplishments. He would have been influenced by the values he held dear, including the importance of education, community, and a deep connection to their Jewish heritage. His passing marked a poignant moment for Howard and their family, as they navigated the loss of a beloved father and figurehead.

Arthur's burial in Beth Israel Cemetery serves as a reminder of his contributions to the Jewish community and the memories cherished by those who loved him. The cemetery, a resting place for many who shared similar roots, reflects a rich history and a commitment to preserving their heritage. Even in death, Arthur remains a part of that continuum, his life story woven into the fabric of the community he held dear. His legacy lives on in Howard and those who remember him fondly, embodying the values he instilled and the love he shared.

Rita (Turk) Intrator[11]

R ita nee Turk was born in 1928 into a world still recovering from the aftermath of World War I and witnessing the rise of new social and political dynamics. In the late 1920s, many countries were experiencing economic upheaval, setting the stage for the Great Depression that would soon follow in 1929. For Jewish communities, the late 1920s were marked by both hope and uncertainty. The optimism of the postwar era was tempered by rising anti-Semitic sentiments in various parts of the world, particularly in Europe, as they began to see the seeds of unrest that would lead to more dire circumstances in the 1930s.

In this atmosphere, Rita's early years would have been shaped by a strong sense of family and community. Jewish traditions and values would have played a central role in her upbringing, providing a sense of identity and belonging during a time of change.

The 1930s would bring challenges, including economic hardship and the threat of totalitarian regimes in Europe. Despite these struggles, Rita would likely have experienced a childhood filled with cultural richness, celebrating Jewish holidays, participating in community events, and building relationships with family and friends that would be the foundation of her life.

Rita would have been a teenager during World War II, a period that would profoundly impact her worldview. The war brought significant upheaval, forcing many Jewish families to confront the harsh realities of life under Nazi rule and the broader impacts of the Holocaust. Yet, despite these tribulations, the resilience of the Jewish spirit persisted, shaping Rita's values and her approach to life.

As she transitioned into adulthood in the post-war years, Rita would have witnessed the rebuilding of communities, the establishment of Israel in 1948, and the ongoing struggle for civil rights. These events would not only inform her identity but also influence her perspectives on family, faith, and community engagement throughout her life.

Her journey, intertwined with Arthur's, reflects a deep commitment to their shared values and heritage, which would serve as a guiding light in the challenges and triumphs they would face together.

RITA NEE TURK WAS 29 years old when the Soviet Union launched Sputnik on October 4, 1957. This monumental event marked the dawn of the space age and was a symbol of technological advancement and competition during the Cold War era. The launch not only stirred excitement and wonder around the world but also ignited concerns over the implications of space exploration, particularly regarding military capabilities.

For Rita, living through this era would have been a time of significant change and possibility. The late 1950s were characterized by a surge in scientific achievement and a growing interest in education and innovation, especially in the fields of science and technology. This cultural backdrop may have influenced her worldview, as she balanced the thrill of global advancements with the challenges of daily life.

As a Jewish woman, Rita would have experienced the complexities of identity during a time of shifting societal norms. The 1950s were also marked by a push for civil rights and social justice, movements that echoed within Jewish communities advocating for equality and tolerance. This period would have prompted her to reflect on her values and the importance of community, family, and faith, as the world around her rapidly evolved.

In her personal life, Rita may have been navigating her role as a wife and mother, adapting to the expectations of the time while also embracing the opportunities presented by a changing society. The excitement surrounding the space race and technological progress could have inspired her and those around her to dream big, envisioning futures that extended beyond traditional boundaries.

As the world celebrated the achievements of space exploration, Rita's journey intertwined with Arthur's, reflecting a shared commitment to family and community amid the backdrop of a dynamic historical moment. The optimism and uncertainty of this era would continue to shape their lives and the lives of future generations.

RITA WAS 32 YEARS OLD when her son, Howard Barry, was born in 1961. This was a time of great social change and cultural upheaval, marked by significant events that would shape the future of the world. The early 1960s were characterized by the civil rights movement, the rise of counterculture, and increasing awareness of social issues, all of which influenced many families' lives, including Rita's.

As a new mother, Rita likely experienced a mix of joy and challenges as she welcomed Howard into the world. The excitement of having a child during this dynamic period could have inspired her to be particularly attentive to the values and lessons she wanted to instill in him. The ideals of equality, justice, and community were prominent during this time, and Rita may have sought to ensure that her son grew up with a strong sense of identity and social responsibility.

In 1961, the United States was also engaged in the space race, with the launch of the first American astronaut, Alan Shepard, into space. The fascination with science and technology would have permeated daily life, with parents like Rita encouraging their children to dream big and aspire to greatness. Schools began emphasizing STEM education, inspiring a new generation to explore careers in science, engineering, and beyond.

Rita's life as a mother was also shaped by the evolving expectations of women in society. While many women of her generation continued to embrace traditional roles as homemakers, the women's liberation movement was beginning to gain momentum, advocating for greater rights and opportunities. This context may have influenced Rita's perspective on motherhood and her aspirations for herself and her family.

As she navigated the responsibilities of raising Howard, Rita likely balanced her hopes for him with the realities of the world around them. Family gatherings, Jewish traditions, and community involvement would have played vital roles in their lives, fostering a sense of belonging and continuity amidst the changes of the era.

Rita's nurturing spirit and dedication to her family would have laid the groundwork for Howard's upbringing, instilling in him the values and resilience needed to face the challenges of a rapidly changing world.

RITA WAS 48 YEARS OLD when her husband, Arthur Intrator, passed away in 1977. This loss marked a significant turning point in her life. Navigating the world as a widow, Rita faced the profound grief that comes with losing a life partner. The emotional and practical challenges of this transition would have been considerable, especially as she continued to raise her son, Howard Barry, who was in his teenage years at the time.

In the late 1970s, societal norms around family and gender roles were evolving. Rita may have found herself reevaluating her position within the family and the broader community. With her husband gone, she might have needed to step into new responsibilities, both emotionally and financially. The support of her Jewish community could have been invaluable during this time, providing a network of friends and family to help her cope with the challenges of single parenthood.

The late 1970s also saw the rise of women's rights, which may have influenced Rita's sense of independence. As she adjusted to her new reality, she could have drawn on the strength of the women around her—whether through friends, family, or community organizations—to find support and solidarity. This period might have encouraged her to pursue personal growth, whether through education, employment, or involvement in community activities.

Rita's experience of widowhood may have deepened her connection to her Jewish faith and traditions. Finding solace in her religious practices, she likely turned to rituals and community gatherings to help navigate her grief. Celebrations of life events, such as bar and bat mitzvahs, would have held special significance, allowing her to honor her heritage while creating lasting memories with Howard.

As she faced the years following her husband's death, Rita would have shown resilience, drawing on her love for her son and her faith to forge a new path forward. Howard would have grown to appreciate the strength and dedication of his mother, as she worked to provide a stable and nurturing home despite the loss they both felt. Rita's journey through grief and renewal would ultimately shape the family dynamic, instilling in Howard a profound understanding of love, perseverance, and the importance of community.

RITA WAS 53 YEARS OLD when the Canada Act, also known as the Constitution Act, 1982, was passed. This act marked a significant moment in Canadian history, as it patriated the Canadian

Constitution from Britain and included the Canadian Charter of Rights and Freedoms. The changes brought about by the Canada Act had wide-ranging implications for Canadians, including those in Rita's Jewish community.

During this time, Rita may have experienced a renewed sense of national identity and pride as Canada began to assert its independence more firmly. The Canada Act aimed to provide citizens with a greater voice in their rights and freedoms, including protection against discrimination based on religion, ethnicity, or gender. For Rita, as a Jewish woman and a member of a historically marginalized group, the Charter's provisions could have provided a sense of security and hope for future generations.

In the early 1980s, discussions about multiculturalism and the celebration of diversity were increasingly prevalent. Rita may have engaged in conversations about the importance of preserving her Jewish heritage while also embracing the multicultural fabric of Canadian society. This was a time when many Canadians were reflecting on the country's identity and values, and Rita's participation in these dialogues could have strengthened her connections with both her Jewish roots and the broader Canadian community.

As a mother, Rita likely felt a responsibility to instill in her son, Howard Barry, a sense of pride in both his Jewish identity and his Canadian citizenship. She may have sought out community events and educational opportunities that highlighted the contributions of Jewish Canadians to the country's history and culture. These experiences could have served to enrich Howard's understanding of his heritage while fostering a sense of belonging in an increasingly diverse society.

The 1980s were also marked by economic challenges and changes, including inflation and shifts in the job market. Rita may have had to adapt to these economic realities, potentially seeking new opportunities or resources to support her family. As a strong and resilient woman, she could have drawn on her community for support, whether through networking or local programs aimed at helping families navigate financial difficulties.

During this period, Rita's resilience and adaptability would have been essential in maintaining a stable home for Howard while navigating the changes in Canadian society. The passage of the Canada Act, with its emphasis on rights and freedoms, would have resonated deeply with her, serving as a reminder of the importance of community, identity, and the ongoing fight for equality and recognition in a rapidly changing world.

RITA WAS 71 YEARS OLD when her son, Harry, passed away in 2000. The loss of a child is an unimaginable tragedy for any parent, and for Rita, it marked a profound turning point in her life. In the year 2000, she found herself navigating the complex emotions of grief, sorrow, and reflection as she came to terms with the loss of her beloved son.

As she processed this heart-wrenching event, Rita likely drew on the strength of her faith and the support of her community. Jewish traditions surrounding mourning, including the practice of sitting shiva, would have offered her a framework to express her grief while surrounded by family and friends. These rituals not only honored Harry's memory but also provided a space for shared stories and connections, allowing Rita to feel the love and support of those around her during such a difficult time.

In addition to the emotional toll, Rita may have also faced practical challenges in the aftermath of Harry's passing. She might have been involved in making arrangements, sorting through his belongings, and dealing with the logistics of his estate. This process can be overwhelming, especially for someone in their later years, as it requires confronting the realities of loss while also honoring the life of the deceased.

At the same time, Rita likely reflected on the memories she shared with Harry, cherishing the moments that defined their relationship. She may have found solace in recalling the joys of his childhood, the milestones he achieved, and the love they had for each other. Such reflections could have helped her navigate her grief, allowing her to celebrate Harry's life even as she mourned his absence.

The year 2000 was also a time of significant change and progress in Canadian society, with advancements in technology and communication reshaping daily life. Rita might have felt a sense of disconnection from the fast-paced world around her as she grappled with her loss. However, she could have also found comfort in the ways that technology allowed her to stay connected with family and friends, sharing memories and stories of Harry through phone calls or even the burgeoning world of the internet.

As Rita continued to honor her son's memory, she may have become an advocate for others who had experienced similar losses. Drawing from her own journey of grief, she could have offered support to friends or community members navigating their own heartbreaks, fostering connections that helped her feel less alone in her sorrow.

In the years following Harry's death, Rita's resilience would likely have shone through as she continued to engage with her community and family. While the pain of her loss would always remain a part of her life, she might have also sought out new experiences, drawing strength from her relationships and embracing the joy and love that still existed around her. Rita's legacy, marked by her love for her children and her commitment to her community, would continue to be a source of inspiration and strength for those who knew her.

———————

RITA WAS 85 YEARS OLD when she passed away in Kingston, Ontario, in 2014. Her death marked the end of a remarkable life filled with experiences that spanned nearly a century. As her loved ones gathered to mourn her passing, they would have reflected on the rich tapestry of memories she left behind.

Born into a world that was rapidly changing, Rita witnessed extraordinary historical events throughout her life. From the aftermath of World War II and the rise of civil rights movements to the evolution of technology and culture, she navigated these shifts with grace and resilience. Rita's life was a testament to the enduring spirit of her generation, as they adapted to societal changes while holding steadfast to their traditions and values.

In the years leading up to her passing, Rita remained an integral part of her community, sharing her wisdom and warmth with those around her. She likely continued to find joy in family gatherings, holiday celebrations, and the simple pleasures of life. Her strong faith and connection to her Jewish heritage may have provided comfort and purpose, guiding her through the challenges of aging.

As she faced the inevitable decline in health that often accompanies old age, Rita may have drawn strength from her memories of Harry and the love of her remaining family members. The support of her loved ones would have been crucial during this time, as they rallied around her to offer companionship, care, and shared moments of laughter and reflection.

Rita's passing would have prompted an outpouring of love and remembrance from her family and friends. They would have gathered to honor her life, sharing stories that highlighted her kindness, strength, and the countless ways she touched their lives. Her burial at Beth Israel Cemetery would serve as a poignant reminder of her connection to her faith and her family legacy.

In the years following her death, Rita's influence would continue to resonate. Her children and grandchildren would likely carry forward her values, sharing her stories and traditions with the next generations. They would remember her not only for her love and nurturing spirit but also for her resilience in the face of life's challenges.

As family and friends reflected on Rita's life, they would celebrate the impact she had on their lives, remembering her as a loving mother, grandmother, and friend who cherished family above all else. Though she was gone, her spirit would live on in the hearts of those who loved her, a legacy of love, strength, and unwavering faith that would endure for years to come.

Howard Barry Intrator[12]

Howard Barry was born in 1961, a time marked by significant cultural, social, and political changes. The early 1960s were characterized by a post-war optimism in many parts of the world, particularly in North America, where economic growth and consumerism were on the rise. The baby boomer generation was coming of age, leading to a dynamic shift in societal norms and values.

In 1961, the Cold War was at its height. Tensions between the United States and the Soviet Union shaped much of the political landscape. The construction of the Berlin Wall that year symbolized the division between East and West and the ideological battles that defined the era. The threat of nuclear war loomed large in the public consciousness, prompting many families to participate in civil defense drills and discussions about safety.

In popular culture, the early '60s ushered in the vibrant world of rock and roll, with iconic figures like Elvis Presley and emerging bands like The Beatles starting to change the musical landscape. The rise of youth culture began to challenge traditional values, as young people sought to express themselves through music, fashion, and social movements.

The civil rights movement was gaining momentum in the United States, advocating for equality and justice for African Americans. Events such as the Freedom Rides and Martin Luther King Jr.'s "I Have a Dream" speech in 1963 laid the groundwork for future change, while the push for women's rights began to gather steam as well.

In terms of technology, Howard's early years saw advancements that would shape the future. The space race was in full swing, with the

United States and the Soviet Union competing for dominance in space exploration. In 1961, President John F. Kennedy famously announced the goal of landing a man on the Moon by the end of the decade, inspiring a generation with dreams of space travel and discovery.

Howard's family life would have been influenced by these cultural and political currents. As a child in a Jewish household, he may have experienced the warmth of family traditions alongside the excitement of a rapidly changing world. His upbringing would reflect the values of his parents, Rita and Arthur, who lived through significant historical events and instilled in him a sense of identity and resilience.

Overall, 1961 was a year filled with promise and challenges, setting the stage for a decade of profound transformation that would affect Howard and his generation for years to come.

HOWARD BARRY WAS JUST 16 years old when his father, Arthur Intrator, passed away in 1977. This would have been a pivotal moment in Howard's life, marking the end of his childhood innocence and thrusting him into a more complex and challenging world. Losing a parent is often a life-altering experience, and for Howard, this loss would have brought significant emotional and practical changes.

As a teenager, Howard faced the struggles of adolescence while grappling with grief. He may have felt a mix of confusion, anger, and sadness, common emotions for someone his age dealing with such a profound loss. The absence of his father could have left a void in his life, influencing his relationships with peers and family members. His mother, Rita, would have taken on a crucial role in supporting him during this difficult time, and their bond may have deepened as they navigated their grief together.

In 1977, the world was experiencing significant cultural shifts. The late 1970s saw the rise of various movements and trends, including the continued evolution of music, with the popularity of punk rock and disco. The social landscape was changing, with increased conversations around civil rights, gender equality, and environmental issues.

Howard's teenage years were set against this backdrop of change and uncertainty. He may have sought solace in friendships, school activities, or perhaps music, as many young people do during trying times. This period could have also been a time of introspection for Howard as he began to form his identity and understand his place in a world that felt different without his father's guidance.

His experiences and the lessons he learned from his father's life and untimely death would likely shape his values, ambitions, and the way he approached adulthood. Howard might have felt a responsibility to honor his father's memory and carry forward the values instilled in him, including resilience, determination, and a sense of community.

Navigating this transition from boyhood to manhood, Howard would encounter both challenges and opportunities, ultimately defining his path in life as he moved forward in the wake of loss.

HOWARD BARRY WAS 21 years old when the Canada Act was passed in 1982. This legislation, also known as the Constitution Act, 1982, marked a significant milestone in Canadian history, as it patriated the Canadian Constitution and established the framework for the protection of individual rights through the Charter of Rights and Freedoms.

As a young adult, Howard was coming into his own during a time of national transformation. The Canada Act not only changed the political landscape but also resonated deeply with the identity and culture of Canadians. Many young Canadians at the time felt a sense of pride and empowerment, viewing the new Constitution as a declaration of their rights and freedoms.

At 21, Howard was likely exploring his own beliefs about citizenship, community, and national identity. This period could have ignited his interest in social and political issues, encouraging him to engage more actively in discussions about democracy and governance. The passing of the Canada Act might have inspired him to think critically about his role in shaping the future of his country, especially considering the heightened emphasis on individual rights and freedoms that the Charter promised.

This new political climate may have prompted Howard to reflect on his family's history and the immigrant experience, particularly as a Jewish family navigating life in Canada. He might have felt a deeper connection to the values of inclusion and tolerance that the Charter espoused, reinforcing his identity as a Canadian citizen.

In a broader context, the early 1980s were marked by significant cultural shifts, including a flourishing of arts and music, the rise of multiculturalism, and greater awareness of social justice issues. Howard may have been influenced by these movements, which could have inspired him to become more involved in community initiatives or advocacy work.

Overall, turning 21 during such a pivotal time in Canadian history likely shaped Howard's worldview, instilling in him a sense of responsibility and possibility as he began to carve out his path in the world. The experience of witnessing his country's evolution would have been both a personal and collective journey, informing his aspirations and values as he transitioned into adulthood.

HOWARD BARRY WAS 34 years old when Quebec rejected independence in the 1995 referendum. This pivotal moment in Canadian history occurred on October 30, 1995, when Quebecers voted on whether to secede from Canada and establish an independent country. The referendum result was incredibly close, with approximately 50.58% voting against independence and 49.42% in favor.

At 34, Howard was likely navigating various personal and professional challenges while also engaging with the broader societal issues of the time. The intense national debate surrounding Quebec's sovereignty would have been a significant topic in both political and social circles, and it may have spurred Howard to consider his own views on national unity, multiculturalism, and the future of Canada.

The referendum reflected deep divisions in Canadian society, particularly concerning the cultural and linguistic identity of Quebec within the broader Canadian framework. For Howard, this period might have been a time of introspection regarding his Jewish heritage and the complexities of belonging to a minority community within a diverse nation. He may have pondered the implications of Quebec's potential separation, not just for Quebecers, but for all Canadians, and how it could influence issues of minority rights, representation, and cultural recognition.

The aftermath of the referendum saw a renewed emphasis on national unity and the need for dialogue among provinces and communities. As someone living in Ontario, Howard would have been part of discussions about the future of Canada, participating in conversations that sought to bridge gaps between differing viewpoints and fostering understanding among diverse populations.

This period also coincided with significant advancements in technology and communication, leading to a more interconnected world. Howard may have utilized these developments to connect with others who shared his concerns and aspirations for a united Canada, potentially engaging in grassroots movements or advocacy for greater interprovincial cooperation.

Overall, turning 34 during this significant juncture in Canadian history likely reinforced Howard's sense of identity and commitment to the values of inclusivity and cooperation, shaping his understanding of what it means to be a Canadian in a diverse and evolving society.

HOWARD BARRY WAS 39 years old when he passed away in 2000, leaving behind a legacy shaped by his experiences and contributions to his community. His untimely death likely brought a profound sense of loss to those who knew him, including family, friends, and colleagues. Howard's life was a tapestry woven with the threads of cultural heritage, personal achievements, and the challenges of navigating a complex world.

In the year 2000, Canada was entering a new millennium marked by technological advancements and an increasingly multicultural society. Discussions surrounding identity, immigration, and social justice were at the forefront of national discourse. Howard, as a Jewish Canadian, may have been particularly attuned to the nuances of cultural identity and the importance of fostering community connections.

His burial in Beth Israel Cemetery signifies a return to his roots and an acknowledgment of the Jewish traditions that shaped his upbringing. It serves as a reminder of the importance of family and community ties, providing a space for loved ones to reflect on his life and the impact he made during his time on earth.

In the years following his passing, Howard's memory may have continued to influence those who knew him. His contributions to discussions about identity, belonging, and community cohesion likely left a lasting impression on his friends and family, encouraging them to carry forward the values he championed. The cemetery itself stands as a testament to the enduring connections between generations and the stories that intertwine in the lives of those who came before and those who will follow.

The legacy of Howard Barry endures not only in the memories of those who loved him but also in the ongoing journey of individuals navigating their own identities in a diverse and ever-changing world. His life, although cut short, remains a meaningful part of the narrative of his community and the broader Canadian experience.

FORGET ME NOT

VOLUNTEERS NEEDED[1]

1. https://billiongraves.com/cemetery/Beth-Israel-Cemetery/322910/volunteer

[1] https://www.wikitree.com/wiki/Kizell-1

[2] https://www.wikitree.com/wiki/Berofe-1

[3] https://www.wikitree.com/wiki/Cohen-6256

[4] https://www.wikitree.com/wiki/Fisher-19036

[5] https://www.wikitree.com/wiki/Ginsberg-207

[6] https://www.wikitree.com/wiki/Goldstein-1438

[7] https://www.wikitree.com/wiki/Goldstein-1676

[8] https://www.wikitree.com/wiki/Groll-59

[9] https://www.wikitree.com/wiki/Hamburger-229

[10] https://www.wikitree.com/wiki/Intrator-10

[11] https://www.wikitree.com/wiki/Turk-798

[12] https://www.wikitree.com/wiki/Intrator-11

Don't miss out!

Visit the website below and you can sign up to receive emails whenever Angeline Gallant publishes a new book. There's no charge and no obligation.

https://books2read.com/r/B-A-QGSI-YRZDF

BOOKS 2 READ

Connecting independent readers to independent writers.

Also by Angeline Gallant

A Dragon's Diary
Dreaming of Dragons

Calling Her Heart
Whisper of the Heart
No Turning Back
Forsake Me Not
Hear My Cry

FORGET ME NOT
Victoria, Ontario's Babies 1894 - 1895

GENERATIONS OF THE VOLGA
A Family's Legacy

Guardian of the Heart
Fallen Petals

Keeper Of Secrets
A Lady's Secret

Kingston's Love Chronicles
Springtime Promises

Midnight's Awakening
Heart of the Storm
Walking Through The Storm
Walking Through The Storm
Heart of the Storm

Secrets of the Underworld
Deklan's Dragons

Tell My Story Collection
Tell My Story: Germany 1851
Tell My Story: England 1852
Whispers From The Garrison Church

The Dervock Legacy
Echoes of Dervock

The Grave Whisperer
Cataraqui United Church Cemetery
Wedding Bells in Kingston, Ontario, Canada 1923
St. Paul's Anglican Churchyard Kingston, Ontario, Canada A-B
St. Paul's Anglican Churchyard, Kingston, Ontario, Canada C - D
St. Paul's Anglican Churchyard, Kingston, Ontario, Canada G - H
St. Paul's Anglican Churchyard, Kingston, Ontario, Canada J - N
St. Paul's Anglican Churchyard, Kingston, Ontario, Canada O - R
St. Paul's Anglican Churchyard, Kingston, Ontario, Canada S - T
St. Paul's Anglican Churchyard, Kingston, Ontario T - Z
Small Graveyards & Burial Grounds: Kingston, Ontario, Canada
Cataraqui United Church Cemetery 1
Cataraqui United Church Cemetery 2
Cataraqui United Church Cemetary 3
Cataraqui United Church Cemetery 4
Cataraqui United Church Cemetery 5
Beth Israel Cemetery
Cataraqui United Church Cemetery 6
Beneath the Surface: Echoes from Beth Israel Cemetery

The Timeless Veil
Eternal Devotion

The Wolf Whisperer Series
Journey of the Heart
Cry of a Warrior
Wolf Whisperer volumes 1 & 2
Endless White

The Wolf Whisperer volumes 1 & 2

Timeless
The Time Keeper's Sanctuary

Timeless Whispers of Dervock Saga
Secrets of Dervock

Standalone
Winds of Change vol 1-3

Watch for more at https://www.goodreads.com/author/show/
19703964.Angeline_Gallant.

About the Author

Angeline Gallant is a Geneology addict who loves to work on her family tree and help others with theirs. This passion for history plays a huge role in her books as well.

An Old Stock Canadian and a homeschooling mother living in Canada, Angeline is determined to leave her own special mark on the world through her work, her child, and her writing.

Angeline is an author on Goodreads. If you follow her account on Goodreads, she will follow back.

Read more at https://www.goodreads.com/author/show/19703964.Angeline_Gallant.